UNLEASH HER WILD
by Akaiy'ha

A Womens' Guide To Restoring Wholeness Through Ancient Feminine Wisdom

To request permissions, contact the publisher at hello@luckybookpublishing.com.

Paperback ISBN: 978-1-998287-07-9
Hardcover ISBN: 978-1-998287-08-6
E-book ISBN: 978-1-998287-09-3

1st edition, March 2024.

MY GIFT TO YOU!

I am so glad you're here!

As my Gift to you, get FREE Access to Audio Recordings of several Practices as well as Printable PDFs of the Wheels found throughout the book and other Free Resources by scanning the QR Code below or visiting https://medicinewomenrise.com/ free-resources-signup/

Contents

Welcome, Sisters.

Come sit with me in Sacred Circle.

Women, we have wildness in our bones. It is woven into the fabric of both our individual and collective energy. We are Bleeders, Life carriers, Birthers, Healers, Priestesses, Medicine Women, Witches, and Foretellers, and we will continue to be this for eons to come. Right now, we are experiencing a massive shift in soul awakening on our planet, and this is here to help us give birth to greater Love, Union, and deeper reverence for all of Life.

The Sacred vessels of our Feminine bodies hold the keys to clearing patterns that do not serve us, activating our Divine Potential, and unleashing the Wild, embodied, creative, free energy of a Woman who knows who she is so deeply, and never needs validation or permission from anyone but herself. The Creative Life Force Energy held in our bodies, is ours, to use how we desire and has the power to create the reality we dream of and envision for ourselves and the Planet.

Through unearthed Ancient Feminine Wisdom practices, Ceremony, Cyclical Living, Story, and Reflection Questions in this book, we will descend into the depths of the nutritive soil of our Earth Mother, and awaken the dormant, re-pressed parts of ourselves, then rise up into our fullest expression of Sacred beings who are living a human experience in feminine vessels.

Like the Medicine Women Circles and retreats that I offer, *Unleash Her Wild* is for all of us Women who have ever doubted our intuition, repressed our urges, battled demons of shame and unworthiness, and forgotten the power we hold in our Hearts, and Womb Spaces, that can hold us back from creating the life we deeply desire here on Earth.

....

This book that you hold in your hands took a while to gestate, to birth to life. Like all other good things that we humans create - baking bread, making candles, anything at all that we bring into being with our hands and hearts - this process, too, was a time of envisioning, preparing, experiencing, receiving, conceiving, nourishing, reaching out for support, accepting help, and allowing time for it to take root and form shape, so that it could come fully into the Earthly Realm.

For years, I knew that there was something inside of me that needed to be expressed, not just for my own personal expression and healing, but something much deeper was calling me, on a cellular level moving me to share, for the sake of the wellbeing and healing of others, and for our beloved Earth Mother.

Akaiy'ha

You see, early on, life had taken some interesting twists and turns, some traumatic ones, and others that were rather Wild and "out there" - some of which I would have rather not experienced. It is easy to say, while living under the influence of our light-chasing, solar-worshiping over-culture, that all of these events were "meant to be", but, in my view, this doesn't apply to all things.

I had heard the Wild Calling early in my life, but, due to Trauma that was too much for my Nervous System to hold as a young child, it then got locked away, like a wild animal in a cage. This led me to see the world through altered lenses, to make choices which were not healthy or loving toward myself and others. I learned to change or shift my energy to please others, to be a "good girl", to do my best to fit in, and to live a life that was "socially acceptable".

However, the problem is that any feelings that we lock away need to be witnessed, seen, heard, and healed at some point in our lives, if we are to live the vibrant life that is our birthright.

Once I became a Wife and Mother, the past began to affect my ability to live life in the way that I wanted to, and with whom I wanted to. Something -or someone - awoke in me, the Wild Calling or the Wild Woman, the part of me that I had locked away years before. It was undeniable, and eventually I realized that there were some changes that I needed to make to unleash this *Inner Wild* inside of me again. What transpired since then is what brings me to this page, and to reaching out to you, Dear Sister.

For many years now, I have been blessed and privileged to live my life in a way that fosters the Freedom I have always yearned for - the choice to make a living in a way that reflects who I am in my core essence, and the opportunities to share my own healing journey back to Wholeness with others, in large and small group sessions, and in Sacred Circles.

From this, I came to understand that my own experiences of becoming – like those that I share here in the pages of this book - are not actually just my *own*, but also belong to many Women, who can intimately relate to them.

The stories, practices, and Ancient Feminine Wisdom that I share here may stir you in ways that you never could have imagined. They may help you to connect to your body in a profound and deeply loving way, and they may break you free from the cages of human opinion where others - or you, yourself - have locked you away.

From Heartache, Grief, Pain, Letting Go, and Death of the Old, to Ecstatic Joy, Pleasure, Vitality, and Remembrance of all Life as Sacred, this book is one of Reclamation and Integrations of the parts of ourselves that we have buried deep down, afraid to show anyone, hidden out of a sense of shame and unworthiness. It is an inner excavation of the bones of the past, and a coming together in Wholeness and Sacred Union, within yourself, and with those you share energy.

I share the process of Restoring Wholeness in this book, including some personal stories - some that I have shared with many, while others are ones that I have only ever shared with a few - until now, that is. My truth is my own, and I share it with you vulnerably and openly. I do this in the hope that they will provide texture to some essential parts of being and living as Women that are rarely talked about openly; I hope they point the way for all of us to a natural way of being in the world, where we can speak about what have been hidden or negated topics.

The offerings that I give openly here from my heart - along with the exchanges with those whom I've had the Pleasure of walking alongside, holding space for, and sitting with in Circle - have shown me the way back to Wholeness, through a series of "awakenings" to my natural, *Wild* self, a pathway for living my life that is undeniably the most powerful thing that I have ever felt or known.

There are stories here from my own experience of living a life touched deeply by The Wild Woman, to guide you, inspire you, and let you know that you are not alone, even in times of the darkest and deepest sorrow, or those of the greatest and most ravenous rage. My wish for you is that these stories connect you deeply to your *Wild* - that untamed expression of your true being that lives within you - so that you can bring her to life, your life.

It may be that some of the things that I share in this book may feel shocking for you. They will probably rattle the cage of your own inner Wild, beckon you to pay closer attention to your life, and your body.

I trust that you will listen to your body closely, taking from this offering only what it needs right now, and let the rest fall away to the ground, allowing it to become the compost for something new to emerge from it that is uniquely you.

It is my most sincere hope for you that, if something feels alive in your heart, womb, pussy, or any other area of your body - even if it feels shocking in its audacious newness - you will recognize it as being for you, Dear Sister, something that is primal for your own expansion into freedom and sovereignty. Listen to your Inner Knowing all along the way, cherishing it deeply as the beautiful gift that it is. It will guide you through.

With devotion to our Sacred path of living *Wild* and *Free*, Akaiy'ha

What is "Wild"?

In this book, *Unleash Her Wild,* I focus primarily on The Wild Woman, but the sharing here is not limited to her alone, nor to what we think *"Wild"* means in the cultural sense. The term "Wild" is used to give texture to something that is untamed, natural, raw, free. It does not denote a certain idea or image that we may have seen in the media, such as in *Girls Gone Wild,* or anywhere else that society has infused negativity into the word.

To ask ourselves the question, "What is Wild?" is to travel down into the depths of our subconscious, unearthing ancient knowing of Dark Feminine Medicine. It is to travel down into our roots, and see the beauty in the unseen and unheard, but very much felt and alive. "Wild" is a word which can have so many meanings in the over-culture, and can also be so individualized, each of us having our own perception of it, just as we do about life in general.

When I speak of "Wild" here, I am drawing from my own experiences, as well as some references that I feel resonate. This is strictly my view, which I feel goes without saying, but perhaps needs to be said anyway. Take it or leave it, listen to your inner sense of knowing when reading, and feel into your body.

Your body already knows what "Wild" is, because you came into the world this way - with no programming or societal ideas - as a naked babe, ready to suck on the breast of life, and drink it all up! When we are babies, we enjoy life as Nature intended - through our senses, touching everything with our hands, putting things in our mouths, touching our bodies with our hands, following the Pleasure Path that connects our highly sensitive hands, lips, tongues, and genitals to the pleasure center in our brains. We move about life in this natural, Wild way, through the lens of curiosity and pleasure.

As we grow older in "civilized" modern society, we can often stop being curious, through educational patterns that don't foster creative growth, through cultural and societal conditioning and beliefs, and we begin to look at life as if it is an equation: A + B = C. This logical, linear, archetypically "Masculine" way of thinking can be very useful in many ways in our modern world.

However, the issue of us humans feeling disconnected from ourselves arises when we focus most of our energy on this linear way of thinking and doing, of expecting "this plus that" to equal "outcome". We can get lost in the weeds and lose sight of what is truly important when we live our life in this linear way, and especially, as Women.

Since the beginning of human time, Women have been Wild and Cyclical Beings, waning and waxing with The Moon, bleeding, ovulating, growing to fullness in our wombs, and birthing life into creation. The ancient cultures worshiped Goddesses and Female Deities. Around the world, there are artifacts dating back over 30,000 years that support this. Archeologists have dug up and uncovered thousands of statues of Goddesses with large vulvas and breasts, placing emphasis on the life growing and life sustaining attributes of the Goddess embodied. The ancient ones viewed the world as a large female body - the mountains as her curves, the rivers as her blood.

Long before the presence of books, the internet, or outside sources of information, our tribal ancestors observed and lived by the ever-changing patterns of the Moon, Sun, Stars, Sky, Earth, Water, Air, and the Seasons. They were, like us, searching to make sense of this place we call home, asking questions like "What is this place?", "How did we get here?", and "What does this all mean?"

The ancients were curious, particularly so about The Moon and her phases, how she would grow from a crescent to full, back to a crescent and then disappear into darkness for days, cycling through every 29.5 days, never missing a beat or a rotation. The tribes also took important notice of Women and their bleeding cycles, noting that all Women would bleed at the emptying of The Moon, and then be ready, during the fullness of The Moon, to receive the seeds of a man, which they had intuited made the creation of new human life possible. Since our ancestors lived in closeness and community with each other, Women would bleed at the same time, often birthing at the fullness of The Moon, much like other mothers in the animal kingdom.

Our Wild forebearers had only their observations to guide them in making sense of life. It was observed that all of Nature goes through seasons - a cycle of birth, life, death, and rebirth - and these seasons were each like parts of a turning wheel, one that turns on and on, never stopping. The cycle of life became their foundation for living. In order to survive and thrive, our early human ancestors had to learn how to work with the elements and with each other, as a community and culture. We Women were revered and respected as important Leaders in the tribes and culture.

The creation of new life, and its milestones, was celebrated, while death was viewed as a necessary part of the renewal process, and so, it, too, was revered in Ceremony. There were various times that marked an important "turning of the wheel", a threshold, with one season becoming another, the lightest days and darkest days each with their own purposes, the time for growing babies and food, the times for letting go and for letting things die. All parts of the cycle were equally important and valuable, and there was a sense that if humans were to go against the natural flow of life, it would result in a lot of unnecessary struggle and suffering. Paying close, vital attention to the patterns and needs of The Great Mother, and acting with respect toward her and her cycles - never taking from her without asking and without permission - and always in state of gratitude and in awe for what was given, kept everything in balance. We were Wild, just as Nature intended us humans to be.

To be "Wild", then, is to be in tune with the cycles of life that are ever-changing, yet ever dependable in their change. It is to embrace beauty and life, as well as chaos and death, to allow oneself to surrender to the flow of the river, going wherever the current goes. To live wildly is to live attuned to the instincts of the animal body, the Pleasure, Joy, Heartache, and Grief - the full spectrum of emotions, and a sense of pride in the interconnectedness or Oneness of all of Life. To be Wild is to be in touch with deep, creative expression, to Love deeply, to give all of yourself to the moment in front of you, and to be aware of, and aroused by, the shifting current beneath it all.

When I began to write, as can often be the case with creative endeavours, life brought me the insights that I needed, helped me remember the stories, and gave me the experiences of sitting with hundreds of Women and hearing their stories, the recounting of their daily challenges and desires as Women, Mothers, Partners, Healers, and Wild Women. I began to see beneath the surface of my own story, and into a shared experience with Women all over the planet.

We are currently in a time of massive shifts on Planet Earth, and so many people are finding their way forward by going backward toward the beginning for guidance. "Rewilding" is a return back home to our natural instincts and to ways of being in reciprocity with the Earth, our Mother. Just as in ancient times, as well as in the industrial and technological times of plunder, the way Women will be treated in future will be reflection of the way humans treat the Great Mother. The emergence of rewilding is a call to action for all of us, for Women and Mother Earth to be treated with Respect, Reciprocity, and Gratitude, and all Men and all

Women to finally be seen and treated as equals.

In order to take us back on the path of "rewilding"and sustainable living, I share many practices here along with stories and musings of the Wild Feminine to give some context and to bring a new perspective to the conversation so we can all find our way back to Wholeness and Reciprocity together.

Awhoo awhooo awhooooooo.........

If you thought you just heard a wolf howling in unison inside of you when you read that, then this book is for you, Sister!

The journey of the Wild Woman is often one traveled by those Women who feel outcast due to their actions, words, decisions, and life path. It is often a path walked by Women who are free thinkers, and yet may also carry a lot of Trauma and wounds from their past. It is for those of us, regardless of what has happened to us, or through us, who are ready to take a big step forward in reclaiming our bodies as our own, and a heart full of courage to lead the life that we've always dreamed of.

I welcome you here, Sister. I honour the journey that brought you here, and I am excited to embark on this path of Sacred Remembrance with you.

The Wild and Cyclical Moon

Women's cycles and lives are intimately connected to the cycles of the Wild Moon. We have always been, and we remain, in relation with her, even if we are not aware of it, even if we have no interest in examining this relation. It simply exists as a fact of life. We are magnetically connected to her – conceiving, creating, and birthing by her rhythms.

Before we go deeper into the natural state of Women's Wild and Cyclical Being, we may benefit from a quick primer of facts about The Moon's Wild and cyclical state, as well.

- The Moon and the Earth are in an interdependent, permanent arrangement of rotation between the seas of the Earth and mass of the Moon.
- The Moon orbits or circles around the Earth once every 29.5 days.
- The Moon is always there, but just not always visible.

- We only ever see one side of The Moon, as a result of the Moon rotating on its axis for the *exact amount of time* that it takes for it to orbit around the Earth.
- We cannot see The Moon when she is in the phase of The Dark Moon, a phase preceding New Moon, because, at that time, the Moon is between the Sun and the Earth. This first phase which combines New Moon and Dark Moon lasts for 7 days and 9 hours.
- After the complete darkness of the Dark Moon, what we see as the right-hand side begins to be visible first; this is known as the Waxing Crescent Moon, which, like the other phases, lasts for 7 days and 9 hours.
- Once the Moon is completely visible, it is known as the Full Moon. This phase lasts for 7 days and 9 hours.
- As the Moon moves towards the Dark Moon again, it is called the Waning Crescent Moon, with the left-hand side shining the light of the Sun back to Earth. This phase, too, lasts for 7 days and 9 hours.
- The Moon goes through 13 of these cycles from New Moon, through Waxing Moon to Full Moon, through Waning Moon to Dark Moon, and back to New Moon again each year. Our current calendar of 12 months has replaced a lunar calendar of 13 cycles which many in-digenous cultures still live by and observe to this day.

What do all of these facts about the Moon mean when it comes to our experience as Spirit in Earth Form here on Earth? And how is the Moon reflective of the experience of being a Woman? What can she teach us?

The Moon, as is life, is constantly changing, and we are

constantly changing. So, we can expect both, and prepare for both. We can choose to be fluid, go with the flow, and be supple, instead of resisting.

While The Moon is constantly changing, her cycles are predictable because they move from one phase to the next. Our monthly bleeding cycles are meant to be predictable, in sync with her cycle. We are also in the cycle of life, with predictable next stages.

- She inspires a sense of wonder, awe, and mystery, and she can deeply touch our hearts. There are things that are beyond our grasp, things that we can never see, can never know, and that is okay. Living with the questions is just as worthy as seeking the answers.
- In dark times, her cool, dark energy points to the preciousness of life.
- She connects to waters on Earth, to the ebb and flow of tides, to the humans who are mostly comprised of water, and especially to us Women, our Wombs ebbing and flowing, swelling and releasing, monthly – or "moonthly" with her cycle.
- She has shared her power with Women for thousands of years. We Women know that we can ride our inner fluidity like a wave.

Women, especially Women in touch with their Wild, know all about cycles and change - inside of our Wombs, within our Hearts, and in our Yonis (meaning Sacred Space or Passageway in Sanskrit for our Pussy) – and how this can impact our external physical world, and our relations.

Women are magnetically connected to Sister Moon - flowing, ebbing, conceiving, creating, and birthing by it - not only our human children, but our creative projects, as well.

We know what it is to have an idea show up and follow it through to fruition, then to let go of what remains after harvest, composting the rest into fertile soil, and to be reborn anew in the spring after a long winter's rest. Women are Birthers, Water Carriers, Medicine Makers, Weavers of baskets and stories, Goddesses of the earthly realm, Priestesses of the spaces between this world and the others, Healers in every home, Mothers, Daughters, Lovers, and Creative Beings. Women's bodies are receptors for life, the space where birth and death occur each month, physically and in the spirit realm, in the realm of creative possibility. We Women know deep in our bones that change is coming when it is near; we can feel the energy beyond words, through a rush of tingles in our bodies, or when we feel closed or open like a flower to the sun. We carry in our blood a remembering of what was, and a compass on how to restore to balance.

Our Wild ancients witnessed the symbiotic nature of all of life interacting through a dance of polarity between Feminine and Masculine. We had viewed the Earth as Mother, and the sky as Father, while the Moon represented Feminine energy, and Sun represented Masculine energy. Balance and harmony was achieved in these early tribes through the intertwined, interdependent balance of these two energies.

The egalitarian, matrilineal tribes of Mother Earth began to be overtaken by Masculine energy about 7,000 to 12,000 years ago, which has been traced back to agriculture and the formation of the idea of private property. Women and their children became property, denigrated and dominated. All things associated with Feminine energy were thought to be inferior.

In our current times, humanity is experiencing enormous, overwhelming, collective pain as a result of the damage that has been done by the oppressive imbalance of Masculine energy.

However, there is an emergence happening on our planet now, an unearthing of a New Era where the Feminine, and specifically, The Dark Feminine, is reemerging and making herself known once more. She is a disrupter of all that is pretty, nice, and complacent, of all that seeks to take and not give back, of everything and everyone that is out of balance with the Earth's natural rhythms and cycles. Her medicine is alive in us Women, and, like the tides of the ocean, she is endless in her cycles. Since the dawn of time, she has been ebbing and flowing. Her heart never stops beating. It beats in our Wombs, and it is the drumbeat that connects us all on Earth. There is so much war and disharmony on our planet, because she has been buried, her temples destroyed, her statues taken down, and her stories rewritten, with the characters changed to serve a few, to enslave many. But as she has taught us to remember that all things are cyclical, she is being re-birthed NOW.

The seemingly random acts of natural, along with human-made devastation happening around our world, and the rise of disease, mental illness, family conflicts, suicide, and toxic disregard for human, animal, and plant life, has led us to this moment of reckoning. We are being shown the consequences to our collective actions; we are not living in Reciprocity with her any longer, and she is waking us up!

Women, we know her, the Dark Feminine, deeply.

She whispers to us when we know something isn't right, when we feel something is "off", but we choose to deny her warning, and listen to others, or to our conditioned minds anyway. She whispers at first, and then she talks louder, and louder, and eventually shouts at us - in the form of a wake-up call, an illness, a divorce, a breakdown, a death, an ending, a call for help. She has been waiting to come back out and play, to frolic with Wild abandon in the woods of our deepest desires and belonging.

When a Woman forgets her Cyclical Nature, and begins to live in a linear fashion with her energy focused solely on the exterior of her life, placing primary focus on her Yang/Masculine energy, she shifts into a different gear; things may feel like they are moving too fast for her to find her grounding and her center. She may feel like she is losing herself in the abyss of confusion and turmoil, or getting caught up in living her life as others would wish her to, pleasing and fawning, while forgetting where her true Power resides.

When we "re-member" her, and call back the parts of ourselves that have been discarded or tossed aside, hidden away, denied, and forgotten, we begin to live in harmony with Nature once again, and our bodies say THANK YOU.

We feel whole, alive, free, *Wild!* We can easily access our Pleasure and Joy, and we are able to create a life beyond what has once been only our wildest dreams. We stop living in our heads and remember the wisdom of our Hearts, our Wombs, and our Yonis - the wisdom that has been forgotten but is awaiting our return back Home.

We are here to uncover this wisdom and breathe life back into it, to renew it and imbue it with our own Magick, integrating what once was and what is to be.

We are the Medicine we've been waiting for.

The Triple Moon Goddess and the Four Seasons

For thousands of years, the Triple Moon Goddess was worshiped as a guiding force of inspiration and vitality for both Women and Men. Ancient civilizations would observe the Moon's cycles, and would alter their patterns of hunting and gathering, and much later, growing food, based on its cycles.

There were three distinct parts of the cycle, or Wheel of Life, that were observed and each was given a name that reflected a Woman's life cycle - The Maiden, The Mother, and The Crone or Wise Woman.

The first third of this wheel was The Maiden, the part of a young Woman's life until she became a Mother, and it was represented by the New Moon part of the Moon's cycle.

The Mother made up the second third of the wheel. She was represented by the Full Moon phase, that part of a Woman's life after she gave birth to her first child and before she reached the final phase of life.

Finally, the final third phase of the wheel or cycle was represented by The Crone (also known as The Wise Woman), who resided throughout the period of the Dark

Moon, when The Moon would seem to disappear. A Woman entered her Crone phase when she stopped bleeding, when she could no longer become pregnant.

The Triple Moon Goddess, and her relation to the cycles of Nature, still ring true to this day, but observations and ideas have also evolved, giving birth to a new wheel known as the Four Seasons of a Woman's life. This is accompanied by four Archetypal forms that represent each season - both inner and outer, macro and micro.

In this slightly altered view, Women begin life in The Maiden phase of Spring, and move through four phases or seasons throughout their lives, next passing through The Mother phase of Summer, then through the Autumn phase of the additional archetype of The Wild Woman, and finally into The Crone (or The Wise Woman) phase of Winter. This is the macro or larger cycle of her lifetime; these four seasons shape the outline of her life, each one building on the previous one, adding richness and depth to her life and to her bodily experience. There is no set amount of time that a

Woman stays in any season before moving on; it is all determined by her own knowing and readiness to move forward.

A Woman's bleeding years rest usually between the Maiden phase and the Wild Woman and this creates her micro cycle, often referred to as her "Moon Cycle". Her menstruating body goes through these four seasons during each cycle – her inner micro cycle - just as the Moon transitions through her own four quarters each month, as we looked at earlier.

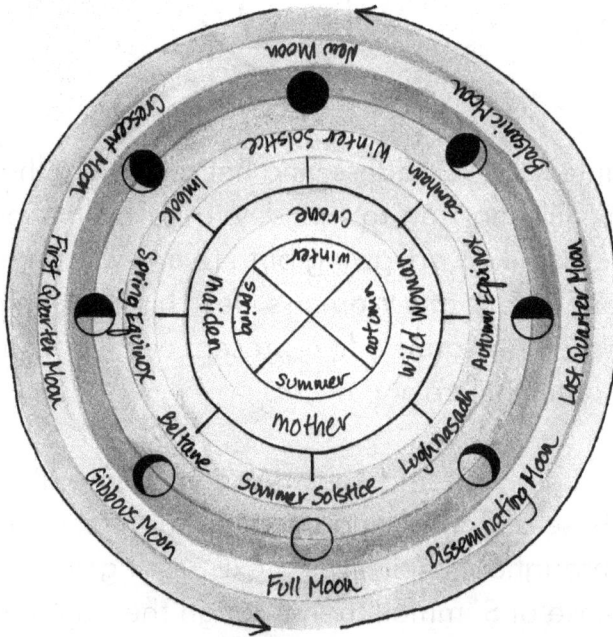

*In addition to the four seasons or quarters, the ancient peoples of Celtic Europe observed an additional four cross-quarters which reside between the seasons as important Holy-days or Sabbats. There are eight Sabbats in a year, each focussed on the relation between Sun & Moon and providing guidance for living in harmony with the seasons and Earth.

It is important to note the added archetype of The Wise Woman, which arose out of a need to bring greater "inner-standing" and wisdom back to the Earth through women and respect for their bodies. It used to be that, once Women were considered done with having children or mothering, we were expected to resign ourselves to the life of The Crone, who was popularly viewed by the over-culture to be denigratingly barren, dried up, no longer useful to men and society, and therefore, invisible, forgettable, and disposable. As many views are changing about Women's roles in society and in their families, there is a greater movement than ever before for Women in the Wild Woman years to return to their own interests and focus on their well-being after their intensive period of mothering.

The season of Autumn is one of letting go, transition, and heightened intuition, as the veils between this world and the Spirit Realm become thinner, allowing one to see more clearly what lies beyond, and to communicate with greater ease. In a Woman's macro cycle of life, this phase occurs closer to the end of her mothering years, finishing when she fully embraces the Crone and her Wisdom. A Woman can feel that she is in this phase for a short time in her life cycle or for many years, even after she is well past her moon-pause (menopause) phase.

Even when she has moved knowingly into her Crone, she will always remain a cyclical being with a micro or inner cycle, in concert with the Moon, and will embody Maiden, Mother, and Wild Woman throughout the Moon cycle.

In a Woman's micro or monthly cycle - "monthly" origi-
nally meaning "by the moon"- she is most in her Wild
Woman or Inner Autumn phase, in the days between ovulation and the onset of bleeding - also known as the Luteal
Phase. This typically lasts 7-10 days for most Women, and is
a time of Magick and Transformation - if it is not stifled or
repressed.

Our modern over-culture (and, more specifically, patriarchal western medicine) have unfairly pointed to the pathol-
ogy of "symptoms" associated with this phase, naming it as
a syndrome called "Pre-Menstrual Syndrome", or "PMS",
greatly influencing how we view what is a Sacred time for
Women - as a time of sickness, rather than as a time of
Power. Is it really a syndrome that needs to be "fixed" by the
male-valued medical system, or is it simply a sign that
Women are out of alignment with the natural tides, and the
ways of being the Woman that she truly is?

For many Women, the phase of Inner Autumn leading up
to bleeding is a time of great discomfort, pain, emotional
distress, and burnout. We live in a time when Women are
doing so much, pushing ourselves to "succeed" in the system more than ever before, and even often stepping into
the roles of both Mother and Father. We don't have ade-
quate support systems available to give us the space we require to rest and to receive, to prepare for bleeding time,
and to honour the needs of our inner seasons as they come
and go.

The Wild Woman archetype is a crucial one for Women

to pay attention to and embody at this time in our Earth's her-story. She has become instrumental in the massive re-awakening of the Goddess, and lives in the gap between we Women doing as we are told to be seen as "acceptable" by societal, religious, and cultural standards, and what we have been made to hide away out of fear. Wild Woman is Sister to many: Enchantress, Witch, Priestess, Healer, Medicine Woman, Lilith, Hekate, Kali, and Inanna, to name a few. She embodies both the wisdom of the old ways that we want to take with us as we move forward, and the wishes and visions that we hold in our hearts for the Earth and her inhabitants in future, that we may live in harmony.

Akaiy'ha

The Maiden

The Seedling

The day is good
The day is true
The day is honest
The day is new

The Maiden is usually seen as the first part of the cycle - both first in our lifetime, and first in our menstrual cycle - following bleeding that, for most Women, lasts between 7-10 days, and is the precursor to new beginnings.

The Maiden energy is most associated with that of the New Moon and Waxing Moon, and represents the follicular phase of our menstrual cycle, when the hormones responsible for outward-giving energy and taking care of others, begin to rise (eventually peaking in the Mother phase).

In our life cycle, or macro cycle, we are considered to be in our Maiden energy up until our first child is born, or when our attention is mostly focused outward on giving to others and taking care of their needs. (This looks different for each Woman and can ebb and flow, depending on where she is at in her inner seasons during her bleeding years.) Until then, she is ripe with Maiden energy - the seedling who dreams of being a flower. The Maiden energy is Spring energy, seeding the potential of what is to come into the subconscious soil of the mind, heart, and womb. She represents all that is new, and her presence is palpable during our youth.

The Spring Maiden will usher us into the next phase, The Summer Mother phase of life, during ovulation or the Full Moon.

First Moon

I bled for the first time when I was 11. It came during summer break. I remember a phone call weeks before with some girls from school; they were talking about how many of them had bled before me, and I was so ready for mine. Weeks later, my first blood arrived. Feeling both excited and shocked, I didn't know what to do. I rolled up some toilet paper and stuffed it in my underwear. How was I going to tell my mother? With a full house, it was hard to ever have my mother alone, and, even if I could manage it, Mother and I didn't talk about our bodies with each other, so this news felt awkward to bring up. A couple of days later, while in the grocery store with my Mom and one of my four brothers, I noticed the pads on the shelf as we were passing them in the aisle, and blurted out to my mother, "I need those!!", but I didn't want my brother to see. My mother did her best to not make a big deal of it, and discreetly put them in the cart. Her reaction seemed appropriate for the grocery store, and yet there was a yearning for more, a celebration of some kind that I felt was missing, like when you know you need something else, but aren't sure how to articulate it or ask for it.

Reflections

- What is your memory of the first time that you bled – your First Moon? Was it a positive or negative one?

- How was this news received by your mother, family, community? Was it celebrated?

- If you could go back to this time, is there anything you would do differently? What would you do, or have others do for you?

- What is your relation to your bleeding time now? How do you honour this sacred time and celebrate it?

- If you're beyond bleeding, how are you honouring this phase? What do you do to honour The Crone wisdom in your body and life?

Reviving the Ceremony of Menarche

In Ancient Tribes, Ritual and Ceremony were an intrinsic part of life, honouring the seasons, and offering blessings. When a young Woman bled for the first time, it was seen as a rite of passage, and was often celebrated with a Circle of Women gathering to honour this important transition through seasons and veils known as the Menarche, First Moon, or First Blood (among other names).

In *Mysteries of the Dark Moon*, Demetra George shares, "Menarche symbolizes the innocence, hope, and optimism of a young girl who is now beginning to come into her menstrual power. In ancient cultures, and those today which remember fragments of the old ways, the occasion of a girl's first blood was celebrated by a ceremonial ritual, and she was then feted and gifted by the community....Menarche indicates that the cycle of ovulation and menstruation has begun to operate in a young woman's body, which now has the capacity to conceive a child....The flow of her blood also signifies that the currents of her psychic energy are now activated, and can be developed. Today this great event in a woman's life is generally ignored. It may be whispered about in the bathroom as an embarrassed mother tells her bewildered and often frightened daughter the hidden location of the menstrual pads."

I can't help but think how our world could be so different if this sacred passage was treated as significant once again.

Would young girls and Women view their bodies with greater reverence?

Would there be fewer (and possibly no) instances of body image issues?

How would this affect the communities that the Women belong to?

Reviving the Celebration of Menarche seems not only an important remembrance for Women, but a vital returning home for all of us, anchoring us into the Earth and connecting us back to the old ways which we carry in our blood. Honouring our cycles, including our First Blood, is the way for us Women to heal our own personal wounds and our ancestral wounds, as well as to ensure that future generations can find their way forward, living in healing reciprocity with Mother

Earth once again.

A young Woman needs a space where she can come to understand that all Women are perfect and whole just as we are. Being seen and guided by the Women who have come before her, who have bled before her, gives her faith and courage to show up as her authentic self; honouring her blood is honouring her Ancestors, and all that they went through, to make it possible for her to be here alive in this lifetime. As the blood represents the full cycle of a Woman's body, this marks the potent opening to her Medicine, to what she is here to offer to her community and to the world beyond that.

There is no right or wrong way to host a Celebration of Menarche. What needs to be remembered is that as Women we know, in our blood and bones, how this is done, and when in doubt, we have our ancestors to connect with, and to show us the way to that which we have forgotten. They wait for us to ask them for guidance, and, in some cases, they are already showing us the way beyond what we can fathom. Wise Grandmothers guide us back to the old ways, while we remain anchored in the time that we are in, which is in desperate need of this Medicine. There may be customs and rituals that have been passed down already that can act as a shining light, or there may be very little to go on. Regardless of this, it is possible to restore what was lost to Wholeness; our blood teaches us this, as our blood is Sacred Medicine with the power to bring renewal and revitalization.

This ceremony can be done for a young Woman once she

has bled, during her first bleeding time, or later on, when she feels ready. It is important not to force ancestral practices onto our youth, who are often so used to a disrupted modernized way of doing things, and who may feel disconnected from this ancient wisdom. It is our role - as Mothers, Guides, Teachers, and Mentors - in a young Woman's life to ensure that the path of remembrance is one of trust and integrity, restoring wholeness.

For many of us who did not grow up with this kind of rite of passage, we are often eager to bring this back to our families and to offer our daughters the ceremony we did not have. And often we are craving this kind of ceremony now for ourselves, much later in our lives, wishing we had the space held for us in this way. We can indeed give ourselves this in the present, regardless of where we are at on the wheel of life; we can restore what was lost and integrate it back into our blood and DNA, healing generations upon generations with our intention and Love. A Woman in any part of her life cycle can bring together her Sisters, Friends, Mother and Mother Figures, Teachers, and Elders from her community and revive the Celebration of Menarche. She can receive much-needed healing for her younger self, who would have benefited immensely from this Ritual. A group of Women can do this together, healing countless ancestral lines, and offering either their blood or wisdom (for those beyond bleeding) to the Earth. Imagine a community of Women reviving the Menarche Ceremony together, creating a new way forward for their community's young Women. I invite you to envision what this could look like for you, your family, and your community.

There are a few ideas outlined below for guidance and inspiration when creating a Menarche Ceremony.

Creation of Menarche Ceremonies

~ Creating an Altar Space (see page 232) with various items representing the young Woman's life in her Maiden years, pre-bleeding. Each Woman attending could bring an item from her own youth's pre-bleeding years that has special significance or a gift to give to the young Woman.

~ Ancestral songs and dances can be offered and sung/danced as a group to or with the Woman being honoured.

~ The blood from the Woman being honoured, or from the other Women, can be collected (if the Ceremony takes place during bleeding time) and placed on the Altar space during the first part of the ceremony. Later, it can be given back to the Earth, a tree, a river, or any place that holds special significance. The blood can also be painted onto the face, womb, breasts, or any part of the body, always with permission given from all participants who may be giving, doing, receiving, or accepting.

~ Words of inspiration can be shared with the Woman or Women that are being honoured.

~ Touch and massage may be offered for and with all who

wish to participate with permission given.

~ Ancestral foods, pictures of ancestors, artwork, sacred medicine, fabrics and tapestries, as well as other items that bring a sense of celebration and wholeness, can adorn the space or Altar, or can be offered to the Woman/Women.

These are just a few of the many ways we can revitalize the Celebration of the Menarche and bring a sense of wholeness back to what is so naturally a fundamental, integral part of Women, their cycles, and to all of human life.

Call on your ancestors in Prayer or Meditation for guidance to find your own way through to ceremonial Celebration, or ask the Elder Women in your family. Be sure to listen to your intuition. You will find the way forward mostly through connecting to your bleeding time, past or present, and giving yourself and others what you feel was or still is missing.

How Hiding Menarche Wounds Women

With an absence of important rites of passage such as the Celebration of Menarche, young Women are at increased risk of falling into The Shadow of the Maiden. The Shadow can manifest in several ways that interfere with a Woman being able to achieve a general feeling of being grounded, connected, joyful, and at peace.

For a Woman who has lived through childhood trauma, sexual abuse, as well as a lack of Elders, especially Wise Women, to offer support as she moved through her younger years, she may feel a gaping disconnect from healthy Maiden energy.

If there have been harmful patterns present between the Woman and other Women in her life that feed into an atmosphere of competition, instead of one that fosters collaboration, she may believe she is beyond needing to go through the process of becoming, that there is nothing to learn from being a seed, and wish she were in a later phase of her life (Mother, Wild Woman, or Crone), earlier than she is ready for it.

When a young Woman in her Maiden phase tries to bypass natural processes, she will inevitably stunt her growth. Her eager approach to life can both help her and hold her back from reaching her ultimate potential. If she is in a rush to become the flower or tree that she is destined to be, she will miss out on vital parts of the journey to get there, life will pass her by, and by the time she becomes a flower, she may not even notice or be present for the grand unfolding.

On the other hand, if she is open to learning from Women who have come before her, and hearing their life stories, she will set herself on a path that is fortified with the wisdom and strength of the forest around her. When Maiden energy is attuned to an open heart, it brings with it an inspiration for the future, a promise of carrying on traditions while weaving in what is alive in this moment, in this world today; it is a bridge between the past and present.

It is no accident that the Spring Maiden is the archetype that the patriarchal over-culture is most accepting and desiring of us females in this part of our life cycle. Being endearingly fresh, sweet, and innocent, as well as naïve, trusting, impressionable, and often more controllable, predators - emotionally stunted and morally bankrupt humans – salivate over this juicy, easy fruit, and seek them out to satisfy their own means. Maidens, sensing leering eyes upon them, may revel in the attention, or fear it; often they do not know how to handle this power, or understand it, and they do not see that it will come to an end.

Reviving the Ceremony of Menarche, rather than dismissing or shaming this important right of passage in a young Woman's life, creates a strong foundation for her later on- for other notable rights of passage and inner and outer seasons of her lifetime. A young Woman who is honoured by her community early in her life through ceremonies such as Menarche Celebration receives a strong foundation of loving support that reminds her of the Sacredness she is part of, not only at this crucial threshold, but throughout her lifetime.

Cultivating Inner Maiden Energy for Creativity

As the Maiden marks the beginning of the new cycle, her energy is closely related to fresh new beginnings, planting seeds (both literally and figuratively), visualization, planning, and an abundance of ideas. We can tune into our Inner Maiden energy, and allow her to support us through the first days of our menstrual cycle that lead up to Ovulation for Women who Bleed, and for those who are Beyond Bleeding, during the Waxing Moon phase up until Full Moon.

As a cycle doesn't have hard edges or lines, but is, instead, a continuous flow of movement, each day may feel different from the previous one and from the following day. It is important to notice how we are feeling each day of our cycle, so that we can know our energy needs and requirements, and be able to make decisions that will benefit our health and well-being during this phase, and set the tone for the following ones. Imagine, if we do not take our time to ensure that little seeds will have the proper environment to grow in; how will we expect to gather harvest when Autumn arrives?

All Beings, large and small, come through the Creative Portal of Mother Earth. Everything we see around us and that nourishes us comes through her Womb. The Maiden phase is often known as the beginning of the Creative Cycle, and also the continuation of all previous cycles following the first turning of the Wheel; carrying the energetic imprint of

45

the seeds we wish to plant, and those we wish to continue fostering in new ways. The Maiden, and her high creative energy, can be focused and definitive, as well as highly inspiring and innovative.

The Maiden phase of our Creative Projects represents the entry point for actualizing our deepest dreams and visions for our future and giving us the courage to believe that anything is possible. Whether we are wanting to call in the experience of being a Mother to a physical child, or being a Mother to a creative project or offering, it is The Maiden who we call upon to begin this creative process and sets the tone for what is to come. How we plant seeds, the intention we place on that part of the process, and our ability to stay focused on what we wish to create, makes all the difference in the outcome. Not all seeds will take and grow roots; this is important to remember. The Maiden phase can be filled with what we might call "mis-takes" in the over-culture's view, when they are a natural part of any creative process. This is a phase of trying things out and taking notice of what sticks and what doesn't, and expanding our minds to ask "what else is possible?", a great time for finding new, innovative ways to ask ourselves, "What do I want to create?". Often, we can get overwhelmed during this phase with all of the ideas flowing through. If this is the case, it can be helpful to place our attention on the one idea that feels like it lights us up inside, in our Heart, Womb, and Yoni. The body knows the way to birth our greatest desires to life; it is a miraculous birthing vessel of Divine Creativity. New Moon or Maiden energy is expansive and inspiring. Taking a moment and feeling into what is alive for us, and where we can focus our energy during the cycle, offers support and comfort, taking us out of our head and into our body.

Reflections

- Take some time to meditate on where and with whom you feel most Joyful.

- Imagine a life where anything is possible and there is a solution to every perceived problem that could possibly "get in your way". What kind of life would you be living?

- Do you feel resonant with Maiden Energy? If so, When do you feel most connected to her energy?

New Moon Maiden Envisioning Practice

The following practice can be done during the Maiden phase following bleeding time, or for those beyond bleeding, during the New Moon, to attune to Maiden Energy.

This is a space for you to come and practice ritual, and to focus your mental energy on what you wish to put your physical, emotional, and spiritual energy toward in this cycle and beyond. Having a journal and pen close by can be helpful to write down your intentions and thoughts. You may also feel called to write without structure, known as automatic, intuitive, or stream-of-consciousness writing – just letting the words flow without stopping what comes through, free of any judgment (see Intuitive Writing Exercise on page 68 of this book). Or you may feel that focusing your words on calling in certain experiences or energy feels best. Either way, it is a space for you to put your thoughts on paper, and bring them into the earthly realm more fully - the first step in birthing your creative projects to life.

Reflections

- How do you want to feel in your body this next cycle? Is there anything you need to do to support this?

- What is an idea that lights you up when you think of it becoming a reality? What are the steps you need to take to bring it to life? Do you need support for any part of the journey?

- Is there anything that is standing in your way? If so, what?

- What have you learned from past cycles that will help you navigate this with greater ease?

Akaiy'ha

The Mother

The Flower

What is more sacred than a body that has the power to grow life and birth it into the world as the Earth herself does?

During The Maiden phase of our lives, our focus had been directed primarily toward ourselves, and entering into the world. In the latter part of The Maiden phase, we sprouted and emerged, being born into the world that exists above the soil, ready to make a debut, explore, learn, and grow. We may have been focused on finding a mate, channeling this energy to our livelihood, or any other endeavour that piqued our interest. We were not yet the flower fully bloomed, and it may have felt like we had so much to do, and so many aspirations to fulfill in the future that we had planned - babies, work, relations, money, house, health, lifestyle.

Once the Spring seedling showed the first signs of budding, we then moved into Summer, both inner and outer – a time of fullness, blooming, opening, and endless giving.

As part of a Woman's outer, macro cyclical life, The Mother phase is represented in the Moon by the Full Moon phase, and in the seasons by Summer. In our macro life cycle, this phase often spans 20 years or more.

In our inner micro cycle, the Mother or Summer phase of the menstruation cycle is the ovulatory phase, in most cases spanning 3-4 days. This is when we have a boost in both estrogen (our inner Feminine Hormonal Energy) and testosterone (our inner Masculine Hormonal Energy), creating the perfect environment in our Wombs and bodies for seeds to take root in the inner fertile landscape of our own Inner Earth. In this phase, we are at our most fertile, able to become pregnant with possibility, to bring our dreams from the Maiden phase forward, one step further to becoming reality and being birthed to life. We are the river, and life flows through us.

Like the Spring Maiden, the Mother's energy is more Solar focused; in the Moon's cycle, they represent the first half when the moon is growing from Dark to Light, from the depths of the nutritive Earth to the Sky of limitless possibilities. These two sisters, Maiden and Mother, are generally more praised and accepted by the over-culture due to their solar focused qualities of inspiration, abundance of physical energy, and outward focus on starting and growing a family.

Mother Medicine

When we enter into the Mother phase, we experience a death of sorts, in the passing away of the things that had led up to that point. Our energy is no longer solely focused on ourselves, but on this little being that we have created. We leave the comfort of the way things were, just as a baby leaves the comfort of the Womb, and both emerge changed into the outer world.

Birth is both a beginning and a death for the mother and the baby, symbolically speaking. It is the end of what was, and the next phase or cycle comes from that ending. The process of giving birth out of Maidenhood transforms us as Women; we bloom fuller, somehow making room to give even more Love, and yet never diminishing the Love we are able to give out. It is one of the defining qualities of The Mother. As our children and creations grow, so do we. It is endless learning and growth in the season of Summer.

In the heart of a Woman, becoming The Mother can feel like the expression of deep gratitude for the life we are living and those we share it with. Full reciprocity is given and received, with both directions clear. Our heart is like the hive, and our Womb is the bowl of honey that fills from the dripping of our heart.

Mother Love is Primal Love. It is the kind of Love that expresses itself from the birth place of creation itself, the Womb of all things. Mother Love is a feeling of being held while being encouraged to grow, the heart of the Womb, the pulse of connection between the past and the future. Mother Love has boundaries, much like the interior of a womb, protecting what rests inside until it is ready to emerge, and even then still offering every care and protection needed once birthed. The concept of "not enough" doesn't exist, because it is designed by Nature to always be enough - enough for baby to grow and emerge into the world, enough for Mama to prepare the nest, enough to give her the intuition needed to feed and nurture her Earth Body that will ensure the vitality of baby, her creations, and herself through the next few seasons. Mother Love is wildly creative, ever expanding, endless – relentless, even - in the capacity for giving and nurturing.

The Mother is a time of life when greater amounts of energy are available to us Women, our hormones at a peak for outward-giving energy, like the Sun. Our focus has moved from ourselves to caring for others, as well as for our creative projects. It is one of the areas of Women's collective lives that is most acknowledged and accepted by the over-culture, and one that seems to take center-stage for many. It is a time of great growth and creativity, of birthing and completion. Just as Mama Earth is plentiful during Summer, so are we.

As fulfilling and opening as this phase can be, however, it can also be a time of burnout, breakdown, and exhaustion, when we are giving more than we can without replenishment or rest, that is, without fully opening to the gifts of the Wild Woman and Wise Woman (or Crone) which we will discuss later on. A Woman cannot give from an empty vessel, she cannot bloom when her roots are not attached to the Earth, drawing water and nutrients from the soil. When a Woman is not plugged into the Matrix of life that gave birth *to* her and gives birth *through* her, she will inevitably suffer from lack of nourishment and die prematurely, without ever fully living. Our modern world prizes Women for being "Supermom" and doing it all; commercials and media boast Women juggling many things at once and making it look easy.

How is this contributing to our true health and well-being?

How are we finding our way through with so much to do?

The archetype of Mother and the related season of Summer give us a template for bringing our creative gifts and babies to life, without depleting the resources that keep us alive and thriving, just as Pachamama shows us how to do. It is possible for a Woman in her mothering years to give plentifully, and not feel she is lacking herself. It is possible for we Women to thrive like the creations we care for and those we so openly give to.

Our Women of ancient origins knew that, like the Moon, they, too, lived in cycles, that a Full Moon didn't last the full cycle and was only a portion of it, that when she disappeared out of sight for days, this signaled rest and rejuvenation. In the absence of artificial light, our ancestral Women allowed themselves to be led into the belly of the Earth by the New Moon, or Dark Goddess, following her cues and learning from Nature.

In our modern society, Women suffer needlessly due to a lack of community, a village of Women to support us through birth, motherhood, and throughout life's challenges. There are very few spaces where we Women can go to take off the heavy burdens and masks and let ourselves be held by each other and the Great Mother herself. We are in a time of returning to Ancient Feminine Wisdom, and with that, a remembering of the ways that Women used to gather and re-birthing them to life.

Birthing My Way Through

I had my first baby birthing experience at 22. There I stood, naked in the tub of the bathroom in the hospital, 7 cm dilated, my mother and mother-in-law looking at me, and the nurse telling me I needed to make a decision about having an epidural soon, because the doctor was leaving.

I remember feeling some faint knowing that I could have this baby without medication, if someone told me I could, if there was someone there to hold my hand, and let me know I was strong enough and powerful enough to push this baby out without the need of medication. Deep within me there was a desire to be fully present; I didn't want to be numb to the experience.

Both my mother and mother-in-law didn't know what to tell me when I asked how bad it would get. They had 11 children between them, and their birth experiences were of the kind where they were strapped down, told to lay still and be as quiet as possible - easier for the hospital staff and the doctor. I knew that I didn't want that.

The pain continued to increase and became so overwhelming, I didn't know if I could do it. I had zero idea of how I wanted this process to go. I moved around the room, which was filled with family and friends, and eventually told everyone to leave, except for my husband and the occasional nurse.

As the pain grew, I became afraid of it. I didn't know it was there to help me listen more deeply and find my way through. Eventually, the nurse told me, with one last alarming reminder, "The anesthesiologist is leaving, so you need to decide." Feeling like I had failed somehow, I decided to take the epidural. The pain diminished quickly after that. I laid down in the bed on my back, the pain now subsided, with a feeling of relief to some degree, and guilt.

When it was time to push, I couldn't feel my body; I didn't know where to push from, or if I was doing it "right". The doctor on call came in wearing a Hawaiian shirt. He was an older man in his 70's with a Greek accent. I remember feeling grateful to see him, as his presence meant I would see my baby soon, and also unsettled that this man I just met moments before was going to deliver my baby. I felt I had no choice.

My mother was on one side of me, my husband on the other, and I pushed as much as I could, with the little amount I could feel. At one point I was told the baby was having difficulty making her way out of the birth canal, and that I had to be cut open - an episiotomy. I wasn't fully aware of what that meant, but I trusted the doctor knew what he was doing and so I agreed. He proceeded to cut me from the vaginal opening down the perineum toward my anus, about a 1.5 inch cut. A few pushes later, my daughter was born into the world.

The next morning, I was barely able to stand and make my way to the bathroom. When I finally arrived, after what seemed like a marathon to get there, the aftermath began to settle in - the unbearable pain of hemorrhoids caused from the amount of pushing I had done without fully feeling my body, stitches on my perineum throbbing, difficulty urinating and forget about pooping.

The recovery from the birth took months. I went back to the doctor twice, because the incision from the episiotomy wasn't healing and had to be "fixed" by cauterizing the area each time with what looked like a very large matchstick. I experienced what is commonly referred to as postpartum depression, had many issues with nursing, felt disconnected from my baby who seemed to cry all of the time, and felt disempowered, alone, and isolated. It was nine months before I could even think about having sex again, and allowing myself to be penetrated, and, even then, it was painful.

In the months to follow, however, I found myself reflecting on the birth, and becoming more in touch with my mothering instincts as I learned to Mother in the best way I could. Something had awoken in me, a primal energy that was opening me to life in new ways, and I felt a purpose larger than myself growing and expanding from the inside out.

Almost four years later, I gave birth to my son. This time, I worked with some brilliant and amazing Women, Midwives who gave me an entirely new outlook on what birthing can look like and feel like. The primal part of me that had been awakened was never going to go back to sleep again.

Reflections

- Are there any regrets you have about the level or amount of support that you received during the birthing process, either with birthing children, or with creative endeavours? - see under the Creative Birthing Wheel

- If so, what could have made you feel more supported and why?

- When has the birthing process also felt like an ending or death for me? Did I take time to honour this transition?

Creativity and Birthing

Women are creative beings and birthers, weaving cycles of life and death, of beginnings and endings. Our own cycles and the cycles of the Moon are tools for creating the life we desire, for birthing our dreams into reality.

During our Inner Spring Maiden phase, the Waxing Moon phase, and the follicular phase of our menstrual cycle, the Earth's life force energy travels up our spine toward our crown, meeting with a stream of consciousness in our minds, germinating new ideas there, and beginning to form seedlings.

As we move next into the energy of Inner Summer/ Mother phase, the Full Moon and when Ovulation occurs, this energy continues to grow and opens us further, flowing into our heart space. We are flowers blooming. Here in The Mother energy, we embrace our earlier vision from The Maiden phase and feel open to giving and receiving from this heart space.

Then a major shift happens, and the same life force energy that has traveled upwards from the Earth to our crown, and has flowed so beautifully into our heart space, now overflows from the heart, moving down into the lower areas of the body, belly, womb, and finally, our pussy. Just as the season of Autumn signifies the beginning of life in its downward descent back into the Earth, along with the harvest, so, too, do we. Here, we align with the energy of the Waning Moon, the Wildly intuitive Medicine Woman, or Wild Woman, and our body enters the time of letting go - the Luteal phase of our body's cycle. On a creative level, for the next seven to ten days, this is when we decide what needs to go, in order to make space for this dream to come to life, and to allow it to unfold; this is when we need to trust in the process, and to open to receiving the abundant harvest from the seeds we have planted. We take out our literal and metaphorical brooms and we clean house. We remember how vital Ritual and Ceremony are to helping our visions become reality in this phase. We know it is for our deepest truth, and we honour it. This time may feel like the peak of the creative process for many. It is harvest time literally and symbolically, a time when we can receive and taste the fruits of labour. The pace and intention we have set earlier in the Maiden phase, and the energy we focussed on growing our baby, will have an impact on the harvest. If we rush the process or try to push too hard, forgetting that it is designed by nature to be an enjoyable and fulfilling experience, when we allow it, we miss an opportunity to receive the gifts of that season and of the cycle.

Following the Wild Woman and Autumn, during the New Moon or Dark Moon, we enter into the Inner Winter Crone. Crone energy takes hold and we quiet to its stillness; we rest, reflecting on the process we have just been through, on the journey of creating. We know better for the next phase what will help us be in a space of ease and openness, so that we can continue being the creative beings we were born to be, and what this world needs us to be.

We can learn from this cycle how to work, play, create, and rest. This is the cyclical living approach that we can use to create the life that we desire. This way, once honoured by many of our ancestors, and is still lived by today by some cultures, is the way that we Women can give from our hearts without resentment, free of burnout, liberated from feeling overwhelmed. By letting go and allowing ourselves to be led by the creative process, we tap into a well of Wisdom that is inherent in all beings, a wellspring of deeper Pleasure and Joy.

Creative Birthing Wheel: Practices and Reflections

The Creative Birthing Wheel is a guide for tuning into your cycle, or that of The Moon, (or both), and aligning these cycles with your life and your creative endeavours, to support you through the creative process.

Use the Creative Birthing Wheel as a guide to create space for your ideas to sprout, flourish, and come to life. It is a useful planning tool and one that can help you stay focused on what is important to you. Remember that it may not all get accomplished in one cycle; projects, like babies, take time to grow and be birthed into the world. It is a template for following the seasons of your cycle, along with the natural cycles and tides of Nature, to give some structure, and a lot of flow. It can be used as a micro cycle for the 29.5 days of The Moon cycle for smaller creations, or as a macro cycle for larger creations such as writing a book, starting a business venture, growing a community, or mothering in any form.

You can use the Reflection questions to inspire some ideas, or take some time to do some automatic writing, centered around creativity and what is alive for you at this time.

Reflections

I will start by re-asking the questions that I had asked you to reflect on earlier about mothering, but this time, reflect on your other kinds of creative projects, outside of birthing and mothering human children:

- Are there any regrets you have about the level or amount of support that you received with your creative endeavours?

- If so, what could have made you feel more supported and why?

- When has the creative process also felt like an ending or death for you? Did you take time to honour this transition?

And here, further reflections about the creative process:

- What would fill you with so much Joy to offer to the world right now?

- What are the activities that light you up inside?

- What creative projects have you have put on hold for mothering that you feel like reawakening now?

- What new creative endeavours are speaking to you?

Awakening Intuitive Gifts

The Mother phase in our smaller and larger cycles of life is often a time of opening further to our creative and intuitive gifts. It can be a time of massive growth and birthing. When things are flowing well, we are able to intuit energy and the world around us with great clarity, finding our way through with ease.

However, with so much outside influence in our world, it can be challenging to listen to what messages are arising from within us and to discern what is right for us or not. This can cause us to doubt ourselves and stop listening all together. The intuitive gifts of Claircognizance (Clear Knowing), Clairvoyance (Clear Seeing), Clairaudience (Clear Hearing), and Clairsentience (Clear Feeling) help us to tune into both inner and outer worlds, and equip us with the sensual awareness necessary to create the life we desire. These are our Primal instincts that become heightened when we give physical birth to a baby, and when we tune into our bodies, and especially our Womb Spaces and Yonis, during the process of birthing other life forms.

Claircognizance ~ Clear Knowing

Have you ever just known something and weren't sure why or how? It seemed almost impossible that you could know, but somehow you did. That is the power of claircognizance working in your life.

Claircognizance, or "clear knowing", is one of the four intuitive ways we can perceive energy. This happens when we just know something without knowing how or where it came from. Our Guides and Ancestors may speak to us through this sense. Often this comes as a seed being planted for a creative endeavour. This sense can be tricky to accept, as often our self-doubt can get in the way and we think , "Is this real?" We may disregard those intuitive nudges as nonsense, pushing them away. While the Masculine qualities that we all have - those of logic and analysis - are left-brained activities, the messages that come from our deep sense of knowing are right-brained messengers, known as the Feminine Intuitive side.

When our minds are clouded with thoughts and beliefs that we have taken on over time that are not serving our deepest purpose, we may find it challenging to know what is truly right for us versus what is right for someone else - society, our parents, our partner, our teachers.

Doubt and guilt both restrict the flow of incoming Guidance and we begin to lose our way.

When we doubt ourselves and our Intuition, the world begins to feel like a place that we cannot trust to be in safely, and we may grasp solely for logic to guide us. We may get lost in "paralysis by analysis", feeling like we need more hard facts in order to make a decision on important matters.

Guilt arises from making ourselves wrong for having a thought that was innocent and pure in its arising, a spark of intuitive knowledge that was meant to lead us to where our soul needed to be. At some point in our youth, we didn't doubt that these thoughts were valid; we just knew what we knew, and, as young as we were, we didn't need validation from an outside source - that is, until someone told us that we were wrong.

When we carry guilt, it keeps us small, stuck in a loop of revising the past over and over, interfering with our ability to see in the present moment what is arising. When we are stuck in the past, we often resort to using analytical processes to make sense of the present, only, we can never fully see what is right in front of us when we use this approach.

When the gift of Claircognizance awakens in us, the blossoming of our knowing unfolds; we trust what is coming in, and we are able to discern with ease what is for us and what is not ours. We draw from ancient knowledge with ease, a Well that will never dry out, that has been there since the beginning of time. We find ourselves remembering ancient practices as if we have never stopped doing them; our ancestral knowing returning to us through insights that we could not have otherwise known through modern day life. When this channel is open, we no longer get in our own way when an idea that is aligned with our values, heart, and Womb wants to express itself on the canvas of our minds. We allow ourselves to dream the seemingly impossible dream, to reach for the stars, with our ancestors guiding us through this wildly fantastic ride of life. Developing our sense of Claircognizance comes through following the intuitive guidance that comes through before we become swept away in the flurry of thoughts to follow. It can often begin as a singular moment of clarity, a drop of water in the ocean of our minds, followed by a stream of consciousness, then a river of overflowing abundance, guiding us back home to our inner compass.

Below is an *Intuitive Writing Exercise* to attune your mind to Nature's Rhythms and to connect with your Ancestral Guidance. You will need a journal or paper and a pen.

Intuitive Writing Exercise

Intuitive writing is a tool for developing our claircognizant ability, and tapping into the right brain (the Feminine side), allowing subconscious thought, intuitive nudges, and guidance to come through.

This practice can be done for as little, or as long, as you desire, keeping in mind that you may go deeper into it the longer you practice. This is a process of letting go of judgment and guilt over what comes through, of witnessing yourself in a receptive and open space, without thinking about what you are putting down on paper.

Let the words flow as freely as you can, and write down onto the paper exactly what comes to mind - expletives, umms, and all! - which allows you to bypass the logical part of your brain that wants to kick in, judge you, and stop you, not out of meanness, but, instead, out of fear-based protectiveness.

Once finished, you may wish to reflect by reading what you have written, gaining deeper insights. You may also wish to set the words free by burning the paper afterwards, using the transformative quality of fire in Ceremony.

1. Sit comfortably in a space that feels inviting and supportive, where you will not be interrupted.

2. Light a candle, burn some herbs and cleanse the space; you are entering in Ceremony with yourself and your Ancestors (if you feel called to include them).

3. Call in your Ancestors and Guides for support, guidance, and protection during this process. See yourself surrounded by your Ancestors, as they create a circle of protection and Love around you.

4. Ask that they guide you through the process of remembering your intuitive abilities, and of helping you to reconnect to your sense of clarity of mind.

5. Connect with the power of Mama Earth through sending a connection infused with the Love from your heart and Womb to her. This can be done through a red cord, tree roots, or any connection you wish to make. Send the energy of Love and Gratitude down this connection into her. Continue sending this for several minutes as you breathe into your lower belly and Womb Space, expanding in all directions, and softening on the exhales.

6. Allow yourself to receive energy drawn up from her through this same connection. Breathe as you receive healing Mother Earth energy.

7. When you feel ready, place your pen to paper and let the words flow through you, your hands expressing the truth of your mind, voice, and heart.

8. If you feel stuck, try making scribbles, or symbols on the paper. There is no right or wrong way to do this!

9. Allow the words or symbols to flow without stopping what is coming through. Remember this is a practice space of tapping into your mind's intuitive gifts - let it flow without judgment.

10. When the exercise feels complete, set aside your pen

and paper, placing one hand on your heart and one on your Womb Space. Breathe into these spaces for a few moments.

11. Blow out the candle, signifying the end of this Ceremony, carrying the Wisdom with you moving forward, trusting it is there for you to call upon when needed.

12. If you feel called, read over what you have written for any insights, perhaps marking anything that stands out for you and reflecting on it for further Guidance.

Clairvoyance ~ Clear Seeing

When we see visions, colours, pictures of the past or future, this is using our sense of clairvoyance. We see these pictures floating inside our mind, in what is known as our "third eye" area. When our third eye is open and clear, we are able to use this insight to make sense of the world around us, by accessing the images and symbols that come through here. Seeing internally with clarity can give us direction and focus on our life path, and also presents a space where we can tune into our dreams and visions, as messengers lighting the way.

As the downward current of energy flows through our bodies from crown to Earth, so does our birthing channel through the creative process. It is in our mind's eye that we first think and see what we want to birth into reality, followed by our throat, where we speak the words and create the necessary agreements, then into the heart where we feel worthy of receiving this reality, and finally down into the lower body where action is taken and our greatest dreams are birthed into life.

If we are blocked energetically in the area of the eyes, we may have poor vision, outer and inner, and have trouble seeing clearly, externally and internally. We may be prone to making up stories that are not a true reflection of life and of the actions, feelings, thoughts of others, which can lead to creating a drama within our minds. If this is the case, all areas following the path downward - ears, throat, heart, belly (will power, digestion) ,sacral and womb (sensuality, sexuality) and our root of Yoni and Anus (security & grounding, be-longing) will have to compensate by being excessive or de-ficient in their energetic output. In other words, our fullest expression will be limited, and we will not fully show up in the world and offer the gifts we came here to share.

For example, if our deepest desire is to have a lifestyle where we can have freedom of time and location, and we can't see it working out with ease, and, instead, envision all of the areas where we may find challenge, we create a block in the visualization process, and this sends a message to the rest of the body through our Central Nervous System, which is the body's communication system, that we are not safe, and this has an impact on our feeling grounded, and regu-lated. So now, all processes that follow have this imprint in them, and must compensate. Our ears and throat have to be on high alert for any incoming threats; our neck does not feel supported, and may become tight, and stiff; our heart may beat faster, anticipating that we have some extra chal-lenges ahead. Our body will feel as if it is in a fight/flight response, when, in fact, nothing is happening on the outside to signal this to occur. As we feel that we need to rush or spring into action to make this lifestyle choice happen, our adrenals and stomach will begin to work overtime to compensate. We may feel we need to do it all ourselves, as we have lost trust in the process, because we could not see things working out harmoniously to begin with. Our sacral waters may feel like the ocean during a storm, tumultuous and hard to navigate, our emotions feeling like a giant tsunami inside of us. And finally, our Root and Anus, insecure, unable to relax, pelvic floor tight and holding, unable to let go. This is just one example of how we manifest illness, pain, and discomfort in our bodies. Of course, we are each unique and the path looks different for each of us, however, if there is an energetic dam in the currents that shape our view of the world, it will cause some form of disruption in our creative potential and ultimately our wellbeing.

If we have been told from a young age that the world that we say that we see is not reality or the truth, or that what we perceive in our minds is not correct, we will doubt ourselves and learn to fear and distrust what we see, internally and externally. We will believe that we are wrong when we get a premonition about something or a vision of our future selves in a life we desire. We will think it is "too good to be true" and tell ourselves it's a fairy tale.

When we are clear in our third eye, when we are able to offer greater energy and ease to the lower energy pathways and centers, the message gets passed on clearly, and there is a better chance we will be able to bring to life what we see in our mind's eye. When our inner seeing is clear, life flows easier. In the book *Take Off Your Glasses and See*, Jacob Liberman draws a powerful connection between outer seeing (how we see the world outside) and inner seeing (how we see the world inside of us.) He shares about the connection of seeing- how nearsightedness can show up when we don't want to see things further away, or in the future, and farsightedness can be connected to not wanting to see things that are right in front of us. In our modern times, we spend a great deal of time on electronic devices, exposing our eyes to unnatural light, fixated on a screen in front of us. Our ancestors hunted and gathered, spent time outdoors, and had to use their eyes to see things in the distance as well as for crafting things up close. Our use of technology has brought about some challenges for our eyes, and too often we seek medical advice or resign ourselves to wearing glasses and/or contacts for life. We can find the source of what is ailing our eyes and our inner sense of seeing, and, as a result, reteach our eyes to see with greater clarity.

Reflections

- What are you afraid of seeing in your outer world?

- What was your relation to your in-sight and sight when you were a child? Do you see a connection between the way you saw your inner and outer worlds?

- Did you see things that were painful or disturbing when you were growing up? If so, how has this affected your eyes and your ability to see clearly?

- Do you see a connection between how you see the world now and your eyesight? If so, what is it?

- If you were to see everything and everyone clearly, as they are, would this change anything for you?

Clairaudience ~ Hearing

If you've ever played a game of "Broken Telephone", you know how easy the message can get misinterpreted as it is passed from one set of ears to another.

Our ears are receptacles, like mini amphitheaters, their design allowing us to pick up sounds and vibrations in the world - within our bodies, outside our bodies, and further away. Our brains then try to make sense of what we are hearing. Is there danger around us? Is someone needing our attention? Are the sounds around us pleasant or unpleasant?

Our ears work closely with our eyes, feeding stimuli to our brain, and creating an internal movie of life, which can either be experienced as pleasant or unpleasant. If we were told as young children not to believe things told to us by those that took care of us, or, if we believed everything that a parent or teacher told us without using our discernment, we may doubt that what we hear is actually what is coming in through our ears. If we used music as a coping strategy to calm our Nervous System when we felt unsafe at home or in any environment, this may continue to be the way we navigate life going forward to protect ourselves from fully allowing the world in. If the world was not a safe place to be for our ears, and we blocked their capacity to allow sounds in and through the brain, we may be blocking ourselves in our adult life, too.

The throat is closely related to the ears; they are partners. You may have heard that we cannot talk and listen at the same time, or that we were born with two ears and one mouth for a reason. Trauma of the ears and throat looks like excessive talking, as well as, on the other end of that spectrum, an inability to express. When out of balance, we may experience ear and throat dysfunction or "dis-ease".

In Anodea Judith's book, *Eastern Body Western Mind*, she speaks of the throat chakra being developed during the ages of 7-12 years of age, a time when we are often coming into our creative gifts and our expression. It is also a time of pre-pubescence, where as young Women, our hormones are preparing for bleeding time, and an important rite of passage into Womanhood.

It also needs to be mentioned that the similarities - design, function, and energy- between the throat and Yoni are plenty. The opening of our throat is preparing our pussy for opening, as well. When we, as young Maidens, find our expressive voice, it makes way for our Mother, Wild Woman, and Crone to voice their wisdom, when it is time.

When the energy in our throat and ears are blocked, we

may feel like expressing our truth is off-balance, we may stumble with spoken words, or with hearing what others are saying. We may hide, or feel we need to hide ourselves behind a mask when around others, to prevent our true selves from being seen fully, in our raw, open, vulnerable truth. We may turn down the volume of the world around us, and turn up the volume of our own inner chatter, in an attempt to stay safe and secure in our bodies.

When we are open, and energy is flowing well in these areas, we can hear what our Ancestors are saying when we connect to their Wisdom, and what our inner Guidance is telling us as well.

Drum Beat Intonation Practice

Set aside some time for this practice somewhere where you will not be interrupted and can have space for integration afterward with a journal and pen.

If you have an instrument such as a Drum or Shaker, this is useful, but not necessary. A candle and some Herbs for Smoke Cleansing are also nice additions to this practice, as well as a Crystal that represents your voice, such as Turquoise or Aquamarine.

1. Prepare your space by lighting a candle or by calling in the energy of fire.
2. Burn some incense or herbs to clear the energy of the space around you.

3. See yourself surrounded in a golden, warm glow of fire energy.
4. Close your eyes or soften your eyelids.
5. Ground into the Earth by sending a connection from your Womb and Yoni into the Earth, down as far as you can go, until you reach a warm, dark womb that feels safe and supportive.
6. Send the energy of gratitude into her, saying "Thank You" for all things big and small that have nourished and supported you recently or further back in the past.
7. Say a prayer of invitation to your Guides and Ancestors. For example, "I call in my Grand Mother Ancestors. I call you in - My Great GrandMother Ancestors and beyond, all the way back to when you drummed and sang freely, that you may guide me through this process, surround me with warmth and protection, and deliver your Wisdom to me, and that I may receive it fully."
8. Notice your breath for a few moments, without changing it, just being with your breath.
9. Continue natural flow of breath here for a few minutes, letting your body settle and ground.
10. Notice your heartbeat; hear it beating in your chest.
11. Allow the sound of your heartbeat to become like a drum in your heart space, emanating outward, in all directions.
12. Allow the vibration to grow and spread throughout your body, pulsating.
13. Take a big inhale, and as you exhale, tap the beat of your heart on your chest, belly, womb, thigh or leg, or on the drum, if you're using one.
14. Continue to breathe in and out, while tapping the beat of

your heart on your body or drum.

15. You are now connected to your heart's vibration and your own inner rhythm.

16. Now, just let this beat be the background for the rest of this practice.

17. Continue to beat, as you add in humming or sounding out from your mouth on the exhales of your breath.

18. Let out whatever sound wants to come through you, without stopping it, without judgment.

19. Stay in presence with your drum beat heart song, for as long as it feels right to you, without any judgment about stopping or continuing.

20. When you are finished, take a deep breath, place your hand on your heart, and say a deep "Thank You" to your heart and to Mama Earth.

Clairsentience ~ Feeling

Clairsentience is about feeling our way, following the body's signals and impulses, Pain and Pleasure as guides, "e-motions" (*energy in motion),* temperature, and energetic changes. Our body is the vessel for carrying us through this experience of life in a human form - the only true home we have - and has a network of navigating tools to help us receive outside information and decode it so we can move forward with greater ease, choosing the path aligned with our Spirit. *"What have we come here for?"* The body has the answers.

The sacred vessel of our body contains a blueprint for

life, and this contains the keys to integrating our ancestral gifts and knowledge that are held in our blood, passed down through our biological parents and ancestral lines.

When there is a deep desire to know our body through movement, we naturally find ourselves picking up on energetic nudges through the channel of our body's instincts and intuitive abilities.

It is often the case that we are led to the discovery of our clairsentience through injury or pain, which is an alarm signal from the body calling us inside: *PAIN - Pay - Attention - Inside- Now!* When we are out of balance, or learning to bring feeling into harmony, we can find ourselves using our bodies to interpret the pain of others, which is not a healthful way of processing outside information. If this sense is excessive, without boundaries, we can feel life is speaking too loudly to our bodies, the emotions and feelings coming in fast and hard, our Nervous System unable to flow with it and ride the waves. We may feel like life is pulling us under the surface of the ocean, and we are unable to catch our breath. We may take on what is not ours, thinking it will help others somehow, and as a result, attract an illness or "dis-ease" as a wake-up call that manifests later on. We may suffer from chronic pain, postural imbalances, exhaustion, chronic fatigue, or develop what modern science calls a "disorder".

It can be difficult to listen to the intuitive signs of our body's language when we've lost touch with a calm, centered, and supportive Nervous System. We may blame our bodies, and make them our enemies, feeling trapped within, and unable to feel freedom in our movement and physical expression. We can develop a pattern of taking on too much, more than our body can handle. The act of "doing" becomes our only way of interpreting and processing energy, and we lose touch with the synergistic balance between *doing* and *being*.

Conversely, when this sense is felt as deficient in our bodies, we can lack the energy to move into spaces that support and nurture us, and we can become heavy and lethargic. We may feel out of touch with our bodies and slow to respond, lacking trust and confidence in our body's ability and healthy function.

When our ability to perceive through Clairsentience and feeling is diminished, it's like the connection to the main source of our power and energy is cut off, lost, or on survival mode. Losing touch with our power source drains our batteries, depletes us; we stumble through life, out of touch with our instincts and needs, like a forgotten language.

Relearning the language of our bodies is the way to re-sync ourselves to the tides of Nature, to The Moon cycle, and to the ebb and flow of life. Our bodies are cyclical, and when we tap into the wellspring of Nature and her messages, we re-attune our bodies to a rhythm and flow that has never stopped since the beginning of our species. We come home. Our bodies point the way.

Our instinct and intuition play a key role in keeping us safe, alive, and healthy. They provide us with the necessary feedback to interact with the outer world through our five senses, as well as our emotions, urges, and impulses. They bypass the logical brain, and are rooted in our experience of Pain and Pleasure, how we interact with life. When we are in touch with our basic instincts, like any creature in the Wild, we remain alert to life, and responsive. We are not thinking of what is to come, we are present with what is, right now in this moment. With our instincts turned on, we listen to what the body is telling us - our heart, belly, womb, and pussy.

What are these areas saying to us when we are in the presence of certain people, places, and situations?

Does life feel enjoyable and pleasurable?

Do we always feel on high alert and needing to protect ourselves from invaders, predators?

How do we know we are safe?

Pain is a messenger, the body's natural alarm system. Pain can teach us how to be a better listener to the body's messages, how to tap into her cues and sometimes cries for attention. It is common in the over-culture for people to hate the presence of Pain, to deny it at all costs; to medicate, silence, and avoid it, by all means necessary. However, pain always comes with a gift, if we choose to listen. We wouldn't have Pain if something wasn't off. And it is through listening to and letting Pain lead the way to Pleasure that we awaken the body's natural instincts. When we let Pain lead the way to the treasure of Pleasure awaiting us, we spend more time in the body, we come back Home and take our seat in the Sacred Spaces of heart, womb, and yoni. Pain shows us where we are out of tune with naturally occurring cycles and rhythms, deaths and rebirths, the natural seasons of life. Pain gives us an opportunity to come back into synchronicity with life, to stop fighting the current, and go with the flow. When Pain shows up leading up to or during bleeding, it Is most often a sign to *slow down and rest*. Failure to listen and take notice, and take care of ourselves, will only lead to more Pain and more alarms going off.

This sense can be challenging to tune into when there has been Trauma to the body and our sense of physical safety has been tested or damaged. We may learn through past experiences that the body's instincts are not safe to trust, that they are wrong or bad in some way. Perhaps in a religious environment we were told that these instincts were not acceptable to feel as a young girl or as a Woman. This may have led to a distrust and disowning of our instincts and body's signals. When we are faced with pain in the body, we have a choice to make - we can get curious and listen, or continue to push down and deny. The latter, however, only leads to more pain, perhaps showing up in another area of the body, or in multiple areas. Pain can keep us guessing, and keep popping up unexpectedly, like it is playing a game of whack-a-mole with us - like deep-burning fires in a forest that have appeared to be extinguished, only to emerge again.

So, how do we heal Pain?

We can start to heal Pain by getting curious about, witnessing, getting intimate with it, and even loving it. It may sound counter-intuitive, but the other choice is to continue to avoid it, which is usually how we ended up with the pain to begin with. We can do it in small doses, taking our time, slowly transferring power from the old way of doing things to a new way of being, enabling freedom in our bodies, hearts, and minds. We can go into the rooms of the home of our body, and open the doors and windows, letting in a fresh breeze, freeing ourselves from a lifetime of being caged. At any moment, we can decide we are worthy of Pleasure, Joy, and living with greater Ease. We may have held onto a way of being for so long, and then the moment we decide to make a change, Spirit shows up through synchronicities and signs, giving us those options and supporting us through to the other side of the Pain.

A Woman who is awake to the natural instincts of these centers listens to the Pulsation of Pleasure guiding her through life. She knows resting is a necessity as much as play, honours the cycles and seasons, and embodies them. She trusts what her body tells her, and she follows its guidance; she is deeply instinctual in her movements, ecstatic in her dance. She embodies the Maiden, Mother, Wild Woman, and Crone in her seasons, and accepts death as part of life. Her touch is intentional, and she enjoys the Pleasure of physical connection through the Pleasure Portal of her animal body. She is empowered, free of shame, and follows her pussy's instincts. A Woman fully awake to her Clairsentience perceives life through the body, and follows its guidance, trusting her instinctual feelings along the way.

If it feels off, she listens, and redirects.

Being in touch with Pleasure doesn't mean we won't experience Heartache, Sorrow, Grief, Anger, Sadness, Rage, and eventually, Death. We will experience these things as they flow through our energy field; like Pleasure, they, too, are gifts. We can choose to see Pain as a natural sort of death occurring in the circle of life, as the New Moon or Dark Moon phase, where we go to honour this part of the path. In doing this, we expand our capacity to hold space for new beginnings – The Maiden energy of New Moon, and Mother energy of Full Moon - energy of growing, unfolding, abundance, fullness, and Joy.

Womb Massage for Tuning into Primal Instincts

The *Womb Massage Practice* below can offer support to help you to awaken your body's natural instincts, through the feeling sensitivity of your Womb Space. You will need to have some space to lie down comfortably, where you will not be interrupted. Use some pillows and blankets to support your body. Take your time with this process. Go slowly. Set aside at least 30 minutes to complete, and longer if you have the space. The more time you can take, the better. It is recommended to use a massage oil that is natural, chemical free, and free of artificial ingredients or scents. You may also find that doing this practice in a bathtub or natural body of water is very supportive, as water has the ability to help with deep release and is connected intimately with our womb space.

1. Light a candle, and burn some incense or herbs, setting the Intention that you are entering into Ceremonial Space with yourself.
2. Put on some relaxing music, if you desire.
3. Lay down and get comfortable.
4. Place your hands on your lower belly area, your Womb Space.
5. Breathe into the space under your hands, allowing the fullness of breath to come into your pelvis, womb, and low back.
6. Continue for a few minutes, focusing on your breath. Notice any sensations, pleasure, pain, avoidance, impulses.
7. Continue for a few minutes here, focusing on sending your breath into your Womb, and envisioning a warm, glowing energy in this space.
8. Place your hands at the navel area and make small circles, GO SLOWLY, and take your time. Begin with small circles and slowly move outward increasing the size of the circles, moving to the outer edges of your Womb and Belly.
9. As you circle outward, bring to mind something that you would like to let go of, that you feel the energetic imprint of within the space of your Womb. This could be a past Mother-related experience, or anything tied to your creative energy that you notice arises as you focus on this area.
10. Continue with the circles, taking your time, and pausing when you feel tension arise, or energy wanting to move through. Allow any emotions to arise and flow through.

11. Remember to Breathe.
12. When this feels complete, take a moment to pause and rest, honouring what has gone.
13. When you are ready, beginning on the outer spaces of your womb and belly, begin to make slow circles.
14. As you move your hands around your Womb Space, slowly toward your navel, bring to mind what you would like to call in: Pleasure? Joy? Grounding?
15. Notice how it is feeling and Breathe. Take pause wherever you feel that you need it.
16. Breathe as you notice what feels good, and what doesn't, and follow your Pleasure. Remember, this is for you, and you alone. There is no outcome to be focused on; stay present with the sensation of touch.
17. When you feel complete in this exploration, grounded, and more connected to your Womb space, place one hand on your heart and one on your Womb.
18. Breathe here for a few mins or as long as you like.

Mother Hears The Call Of The Wild

By the age of 27, I had been married for eight years and had two children. I had everything material that one could ask for, and on the outside, my life looked perfect, and checked all of the societal boxes.

Something felt like it was missing, however, and I felt trapped. I began thinking that something was wrong with me. I had given so much of myself and my body to my family, to grow them, nurture them, and care for them. I was doing so much for others, and thought, "Is this all there is? All there is to being a Woman, a mom, a wife? Surely there has to be more than this."

I would often think about being with other Men, and I felt an aliveness stirring deep in me, as the urge to let loose beckoned. My body was demanding to have her urges fulfilled, and to quench this seemingly unquenchable thirst.

I was trying desperately to silence the internal voices of longing for more - more passion, more Love, more Pleasure, more Wild. I felt guilty about the thoughts, feelings, and urges that were arising within me. I started to see myself as being wrong for having these urges, and the shame and guilt of wanting more felt heavy as it grew louder within me.

I was doing my best to tell myself that I needed to stay focused on being a good mom and a good wife, but there was something growing inside of me that was getting more and more of my attention. I was no longer a teenager, unattached, unmarried, without anyone to care for, who could do as she pleased with little consequences. NO. I was married with two children, a family, and responsibilities. I felt like I had dug myself into a hole and couldn't see any way out of it. There was both a feeling of belonging and security, and a feeling of being confined to a space too small for me to be in any longer.

The wildness in me had re-awakened and the desire to fulfill felt like something deep within me needed to be let out.

There was a man I felt drawn to while working at the gym. Despite an internal knowing that he was all wrong for me, there was something drawing me in, and at some point I surrendered to it. The guilt was heavy, but the desire to be wanted, desired, and ravished outweighed it all. It was like letting a wild creature out of a cage.

I told myself I could continue living this way, living two lives, and had reconciled to doing so. I couldn't change the fact that I chose to get married at a young age and didn't fully know my husband - or myself - for that matter. But I could choose this. And somehow, amidst all of the guilt, shame, I didn't care. I was going to do as I pleased now, for what felt like the first time in my life.

I thought many times about leaving the marriage, but there was too much noise clouding my mind and heart. I thought about the pain of having to separate our family, and what that would mean, and it all felt like too much to bear. But still the feeling from inside of me kept growing and speaking to me; my heart was beckoning me to listen. I had told myself I could go on like that, living a lie, knowing full well it wasn't going to work out. Little did I know what was to come.

Months later, I attended a large conference for work. It was during the Waning Moon; I was on the threshold of bleeding, and my Inner Wild Woman, who had been released from her cage, was wanting to play. One evening during a group celebration, I found myself dancing in the middle of the room full of people, feeling alive, sexy, and desired by some onlookers. I knew I had a choice in what I wanted, and who I would pull in toward me. I moved my hips, my waist twisting and turning. A dance of seduction had begun, and I was loving it. I saw two men eyeing me, one representing an energy I was familiar with but that I knew I would be left feeling empty and unfulfilled. And then there was another man, Luke, a man whom I respected and had sometimes found myself wondering what it would be like to be with him, not just sexually, but lovingly, as his Woman, his partner. The desire to be with him was so immense, I couldn't deny it.

I set my eyes on him, and every inch of my body was calling him in. He noticed me and moved onto the dance floor, stepping into my world of delight and intrigue. I felt immense waves of wet pleasure as our bodies moved together. Some part of me knew there was no going back from here, so I surrendered further to the wildness in me. I let myself dance with him, and I loved every second of it. I wanted to *kiss him so badly, but in a more private setting.*

The dance ended and the party was over. People were leaving the dance floor, and heading out. I wanted to stay in his energy, and felt another internal push to open further. Something had woken up inside of me on that dance floor, and I wasn't going to let it go.

I made a choice; I invited him up to my room.

Within seconds of opening the door, Luke's lips were pressed into mine, and a rush of energy like fireworks exploded from inside of my body outward, a deep sense of relief and satisfaction filling me. I felt a deep remembering, like something in him awoke some memory in me, like I had known him many lifetimes before. In what seemed only like seconds, our clothes were off, and he was inside of me, a surge of serendipitous, wondrous, ecstatic pleasure oozing out of our bodies and merging in the ethers, Divine Masculine and Sacred Feminine union. Time disappeared as we floated in the cosmic space of Lovers, getting lost in each other.

I felt my heart and body open to this man in a way that I had never opened to any man, in a way that I didn't even know was possible. Something in me had shifted; I knew my heart and my way of being would never be the same again.

I went home, two days later, on the train, feeling a boulder-sized weight in my belly. It was clear; I knew what I had to do. The marriage had to end; it had gone on too long and

I had created suffering for myself and others because I had fought the signs of my body, the wild calling of my heart; the yearning of my pussy. I had repressed the Wild inside for too long, so much that it tore itself from the cage of human opinion and societal conditioning, and went on a rampage.

I sat down with my children's father, told him I was leaving our marriage. Nothing could have prepared me for how that felt, nor for the journey that I was about to embark on.

When I left the marriage, I did not have a long-term plan to be with Luke. I felt deeply in love with him, but there was also a feeling of fear that something bad would happen and it would all crumble down. I wanted to navigate my life and any future unions consciously. I didn't want to live a lie anymore. I told myself that the next union that I had would be honest and open, one where I could be myself fully, and I would no longer hide this part of me, knowing the pain it would cause if I did. I was looking for Sovereign Love, being united with someone who didn't need to complete me, because they recognized themselves as being whole, and me as being whole, as well. I wanted what I had yearned for – a Sacred Union of two souls with the deepest, juiciest Love I had ever known, a partner who was a teammate, lover, and friend to share life with. I knew that the way I had left my marriage was not how I wanted to live life, hiding in the shadows. I also knew, after spending one night with Luke, that it was possible to feel this expansive and openness with someone, and to feel Love vibrating in every cell of my body. And I knew that it was something I desired to feel every day, and that it was possible to have this. Ultimately, I chose myself.

As it turned out, Luke and I decided to live together and blend our lives in Union. I was aware that there were things that I knew would resurface with him, as with any union, as a result of not fully integrating them in my past, that I would inevitably project onto him the parts of my own Inner Masculine that I had not fully embraced. Yet, within a short time, it felt like I had already healed so much in this union, I was able to fully be myself and it was okay that I didn't know it all, or that I still had things I was learning and navigating. Even though I was aware that there would be more to this unfolding, that there would be challenges in this new path, the process felt much like coming home after having been away for a long time. Luke's presence in my life was like a fresh breeze, and I welcomed it. I had answered the calling of the Wild Woman within me, and vowed to myself that I would never quiet her voice - in my heart or pussy- ever again.

What happens when you let a wild creature out?

If you keep a wild animal locked up long enough
it will have no outlet for its natural instincts to play out
It will have no place to pursue its urges
to dance, to move around
to follow its heart

If you keep a wild thing closed up in a room
when you go to that room
and open the door
You may want to prepare yourself
for a wild, wild creature lurks in there

She may claw your eyes out
She may bite you
She could devour you completely

When you let a wild thing loose
she will most certainly dance for freedom

unleashing her wildest
rawest form
the one that existed before everything else

Womb Steaming

Womb Steaming, also known as Yoni Steaming, is a sacred self-care practice, working with herbs and flowers as allies, to help heal, release, and reconnect us with our womb space and yoni.

"Yoni" is Sanskrit for "Sacred Space", and is a portal to our most wild and sacred self. This is an ancient practice that can help with improving our experience of our Moon Cycle by supporting our bodies through the various seasons of our menstrual cycle and issues that may arise as a result of imbalances or pain.

Womb Steaming is a ceremonial practice that can help connect us to our Womb and Yoni energetically, clearing out stagnant energy from past partners and experiences, honouring our sacred space of power and creation. It can be done almost anytime, and is especially helpful during the Mother Phase or Full Moon to anchor and ground, supporting those expansive energies through the root.

If there has been trauma through the Mothering phase to the womb space, such as during birthing, miscarriages, abortions, or difficulty conceiving, Womb Steaming can be especially supportive and nurturing. It is recommended to avoid doing it during bleeding, as your body is already in a sacred process of letting go. Below you will find instructions for this practice, as well as a Plant Ally Guide.

You can do this anytime of day... In the morning, it can be a nice way to ground before beginning your day, and, in the evening, it can offer relaxation and comfort before heading to bed.

You will need the following supplies:

1. A blanket to cover your legs during yoni steam and to keep the steam in.
2. A large pot, with about three cups of boiled water.
3. A yoga block or bolster to sit on, so that you are high enough that the bowl is at the height of your perineum (space between your vaginal opening and your anus).
4. Fresh or dried Plant Allies that you're choosing to work with today (see below for plant allies and healing benefits, remembering to always ask permission from the plants if you are harvesting them yourself, and to bless them with your intentions if you have not harvested, giving thanks and gratitude).
5. A journal and a pen to write insights and reflections.
6. A candle and something to light it with.
7. Smoke Cleansing Herbs (optional).

The Ritual
1. Set your space so it feels safe and sacred.
2. Choose herbs that you feel intuitively support your intention.
3. Boil the water.
4. Allow an intention to arise by placing hands on your

heart and either your womb or yoni, and asking what is wanting to be nurtured, seen, noticed, let go of, and so on.

5. Add two small handfuls (or tablespoons) of herbs to the pot and cover for 5 minutes.

6. Sit on a block or bolster and place a pot in front of you. Make sure the water is NOT TOO HOT.

7. Cover your front and back with a large towel (or two) or a blanket.

8. Sit back and get comfortable, allowing your body to receive this healing practice, feeling the steam surrounding your yoni and the warmth entering you, envisioning the herbs and flowers filling your yoni and womb space, clearing out the old and welcoming the new.

9. Write down any insights that you receive or things that you notice during the practice.

10. When finished with your bowl of herbs, give them back to the Earth - under a tree, in a body of water, or any area that feels sacred to you – while thanking Mama Earth for her Love and support through these healing plants.

Plant Allies for Womb Steaming

The power of womb steaming stems from the wisdom and support of our plant kin and how they are able to lend help with such grace and ease. Let the plants hold you. There are thousands of plants that can be helpful in supporting us during womb or yoni steaming.

Below are a few common plant allies that you may already have in your home. Let your body guide you to the ones that are right for you each time. Remember that plants are beings, just like us, and that when working with them, it is important to acknowledge their support as our kin, and to offer gifts of gratitude and love back to them.

Rosemary

Connects us to ancestors; works well as a base; fights bacterial infections; increases circulation; encourages healthy menstrual flow.

Yarrow

Clears stagnation to help with cysts and fibroids; helps us with maintaining healthy boundaries; used as support during deep inner work.

Ginger

Detoxes from contraceptives; invigorates the womb after miscarriage or abortion; encourages healthy flow (helps with balancing scant or heavy flow); connects us to our roots / ancestral wisdom.

Calendula

Cleanses and minimizes bacteria; helps reduce inflammation, itching, and redness; heals scar tissue and vaginal tears after episiotomy; helps with healing of hemorrhoids; reminds us of our childlike innocence and joy; supports in healing from sexual abuse, especially from childhood.

Rose

Reduces cramps; tonifies tissues of the yoni; decreases

blood clots; moves out stagnation; encourages the contracting of uterus, so, helpful during postpartum; reminds us of our sacred sexuality, sensuality, and our innocence; supports us through healing from sexual trauma or oppression.

Chamomile

Calms, balances, soothes; helps reduce redness, itchiness, and inflammation; promotes healing; helps reduce cramps; reminds us of the power of resting and receiving.

Lavender

Supports healthy balance of bacteria; small amounts support relaxation, while large amounts support enlivening and awakening of tissues; helps with healing of scar tissue; reminds us to take time for ourselves, to relax and honour the pauses.

The Wild Mother

Wild Mothering is an initiatory path for Mothers and Women. It is a calling from deep within that leads us to the forest of our belonging and sets us free from the opinions of others, from rules or regulations about how we should birth our babies or mother, both literally and creatively.

For some, Wild Mothering is passed down through the lineage of Wild Women in their family or community, but, for others, it comes through life's lessons, or when we connect back to The Great Mother, who shows us the way forward.

It is not a linear process, but a cyclical one; it can take time to Re-Wild ourselves as Mothers, and, in turn, to create a new pathway forward for our children and those we care for, excavating what has been lost or forgotten and placing it back on the Altar of our hearts and womb spaces.

Our birth experiences often open us to be able to heal both our own trauma and the trauma of our ancestors, both of which are stored in our bodies - its structures, DNA, blood. They become a portal for seeing into the past, of our own lives and that of our ancestors, and an opportunity to mend what is torn, to weave the threads of Joy, Love, and Unity back into the fabric of our families and shared existence. When we birth a human into the world, they have grown inside our womb space for many moons, until they are ready to emerge. Their entire being and energy field seeds, sprouts, and grows in our sacral womb space, opening us to further possibilities in our own creative gifts, during and after the pregnancy and birth process. With each birth, literal and figurative, we become more in tune with our bodies, and the natural processes they go through, leading us back home to our wild ancestral ways.

In recent decades, there has been a movement toward natural birthing and free birthing, where we Women are choosing how we want to create and birth on our own terms. There is ample evidence and countless stories to support that a medically unassisted birth where the Mother trusts her body and the birth process, fully surrendering to it, leads to an easeful recovery for Mother, and a gentle emergence into the world for the baby.

We have been told that birthing is *supposed* to be painful, and, for many, it is. I was one of the Women who believed this, and wore it like a badge of honour. Our thoughts have a major impact on how our body's Nervous System navigates an experience. If we think we need to suffer, with large amounts of pain through the process, then we will. And the opposite is true, too: If we think that we can not only have a pain-free birth or birthing process, but that it can be *blissful and orgasmic,* then it can be that for us.

It makes sense to me now that Women are not meant to suffer in the birthing process, and I wish that I had known that sooner. Our Pleasure centers in our womb, cervix, and pussy, are designed by Nature to give us not only the natural pain relief that we need during the birthing process, but also to expand our ability to hold Pleasure. When a baby moves from the comfort of the womb and begins the journey downward, they pass through our orgasmic centers in our body, pressing up against them, and inviting us to surrender more deeply than ever before to the experience of Orgasmic Life Force Energy running through us. Each contraction is an invitation to soften further, to allow and receive the current of Pleasure that is our Sacred Birthright as Women. When we fight that current, we are met with resistance. When we accept the invitation to surrender, we can experience the ecstasy in giving birth to new life.

The birthing process prepares the Mother with the resources and energy to navigate Motherhood, the challenges and intuition necessary to raise her young in the wild, so that they will eventually be able to take care of themselves. The Wild Mother is aware of the dangers that exist "out there", in the world beyond the womb, and teaches her young how to live in symbiotic union with the natural world, while upholding their own sense of who they are, without caving into the pressures of society or organizations that do not recognize and support this same ecosystem.

Wild Mothering isn't about getting it perfect, especially in today's world where so many of us have lost connection with ancestral ways. Wild Mothering is about following the beat of our own drum, and not being afraid to do things differently, even if it means that others won't agree, and will caution us against it.

Birthing My Wild Child

At the age of 33, after five years of being in a devoted and loving union with Luke, we were both feeling the urge to co-create and raise a child together. We had just spent the last several years taking care of my two children, building a business at home, and our future together. We shared a deep interest in a natural lifestyle that honoured the old ways, and we were learning to re-wild ourselves, so that we could bring this wisdom forward.

I felt so much more equipped to navigate birth and life with this new baby who was to arrive in December, right before Solstice. I had chosen to have a birth at home, with midwives there for support. There was so much that arose from within me leading up to the day of his birth - excitement and joy, but also doubts and fears. I felt my body was in a holding pattern of not wanting to let go, and I was worried about bringing another child into the world, and having the union between myself and Luke not work out. I was worried that it would end, just as my previous marriage did, and that I would have two fathers to my children, neither of whom I was with. Even though there was a part of me that knew that this stigma was just another societal program for Women around how we should be in the world as mothers, there was another part of me that didn't want to go through the pain of separation and heartache again; I felt like I couldn't bear to weather that kind of storm, and to be without Luke.

The baby felt like he wasn't ready, either. Even days after he was expected, it appeared that he was choosing to stay where he was; it seemed like he would never come out! I felt like this was telling me something, and that I needed to face the fear. When I connected to the energy, the deep visceral feeling in my womb and heart, the grief of what was, and let go of the fear, that it would be my destiny again, I felt a shift, like a let down or release and labour began the next day.

After hours of expelling everything but the baby - fluids out of every orifice, in every direction - I felt utterly exhausted. I told myself it wasn't happening today, and, as illogical as that seemed, had resigned that I was done. I knelt on the bed with my arms slung over the headboard, the same bed Luke and I had created this baby in, needing rest. I felt on the verge of giving up, only I couldn't give up.

At that moment, I heard a voice speak to me as if from another plane of existence. It was an older Woman and her voice felt like a blanket comforting my spirit. She entered our bedroom and made her way over to the headboard placing her head between the wall and me. Her bright blue eyes shone at me, soft gray hair cascading down her face and shoulders. I felt like I was dreaming, yet, she was one of the midwives that had been called in to support. Instantly I could feel her energy surrounding me like a hug. She said to me, "Can you give one more push dear?" I took a moment to prepare myself and felt reinvigorated with her words. I let go and allowed my body to do what she knew how, one last push, and out came our little boy. Instant relief and joy filled my body. Tears rolled down my face.

In the days following the birth, I felt a deep sense of grounding, and Mama Bear Medicine in me awakened like never before. I felt empowered and alive. I felt deeply in touch with my instincts and connected to my wild feminine core, as a mother and as a Woman.

As a child, I had grown up watching my cat, Midnight, give birth to many kittens on her own, on several occasions. Afterwards, she had eaten the placenta, and had nursed her newly delivered kittens without hesitation; she had an instinct within her that had guided her through this natural process.

We all have this in us - this ancient well of Wisdom. I celebrated this remembrance and rite of passage just like Midnight - by being nourished by the placenta - eating part of it, and encapsulating the rest, which provided my body and my baby with what we both needed for the journey ahead.

Reflections

- What is a key lesson you have gleaned from the birthing process, whether it be from birthing a baby or creative project?

- Do you believe that birthing has to be a painful process or that it can be a pleasurable one? What tells you this is true?

- Where have you noticed the Wild Mother alive in your life? Do you welcome her energy or is there resistance?

Heart Womb Connection Breath

The Heart Womb Connection Breath is a practice to help tune into the sacred centers of heart and Womb, and honour this connection. It can help with amplifying the energy between these two centers, and with letting go of what no longer serves.

It can be practiced at any phase of your cycle or The Moon's cycle, and especially during Inner Summer, Ovulation, or the Mother Phase for increased and sustained energy and vitality. It can either be done sitting or lying down, for a few minutes or much longer, and in silence or with music, depending on your needs and preferences. It is a nice practice to do upon waking or before sleep.

1. Before beginning, get comfortable, seated or lying down. Make sure you are supporting your body well. Set your space so it feels nourishing, adding any candles or elements that feel supportive.
2. Spend a few moments relaxing your body, taking natural breaths in through your nose, and out through either your nose or mouth.
3. Place one hand on your heart and one on your womb space.
4. Once settled there, on your next inhale, send energy from your heart down to your womb space, pouring the energy of Love into the sacred nest.
5. On your exhale, slowly let the air out through your mouth and send the energy of gratitude and Love back up to your heart from your womb. Make any sounds or sighs that feel good here, giving yourself permission to follow what is arising.
6. Continue to cycle the breath, from heart to womb on the inhales, and from the womb to the heart on the exhales, feeling the energy deepen with each cycle.
7. When you feel complete in the process, take as long as you like to rest.

The Wild Woman
The Harvest

"Within us there are the soul-bones of Wild Woman. Within us is the potential to be fleshed out again as the creature we once were. Within us are the bones to change ourselves and the world. Within us is the breath and our truths and our longings - together they are the song, the creation hymn we have been yearning to sing."
~ Clarissa Pinkola Estés, Women Who Run With The Wolves.

In the season of Autumn - a time of harvesting, letting go, releasing, making space, purging, clearing out, and surrendering - this is where the Wild Woman lives. The Waning Moon is connected to this archetype, which, in turn, is tied to the luteal phase of our menstrual cycle, the 7-10 days after ovulation leading up to bleeding time, the much denigrated and vilified time of "PMS".

During the luteal phase (also known as our "Inner Autumn"), our hormones change dramatically, and our way of being can feel altered to the point that we may not even recognize ourselves. We may become the Wolf, getting tuned into our primal needs and instincts in a way that is unlike the other phases or seasons. During this time, Women are often unwilling to put up with the irritations that the Maiden and Mother likely would not bother responding to. This is also a time of uncovering our boundaries, where they have been missing or forgotten, and learning to uphold them, as our energy is making its downward toward the earth, leading up to bleeding or Dark Moon time, calling us to listen more deeply and tune into our primal needs. We do not have as much of the outward and upward focused energy of the Maiden and Mother in this phase, which makes boundaries all that more important to maintain harmony and health in our bodies and spirits.

Our Wild Woman is also in the space of the macro cycle of our lifespan, often making herself known just before and after the last of our mothering years, or when we are close to, or just after, Moon-pause, when we tend to feel the Wild

Woman pacing to get out. We may also feel her alive and active in our lives when we are about to go through a major "letting go" phase preceding a loss or "death" such as a sep-aration or divorce, a change in career, or a health crisis. Dur-ing the time in our cycle and in our lives where we often learn what we DON'T want in our lives - so that we get clear on what we DO want – this is the Wild Woman. Each cycle, as she reappears and guides us through the process of trans-formation that comes with her energetic imprint, we are be-ing shown how to Love ourselves more deeply, and how to navigate loss and death as natural parts of the cycle, and ul-timately Change.

The Wild Woman is the untamed part of Women, in a world apart from the over-culture, untouched by and chal-lenging social paradigms held up by the long-accepted pa-triarchal ideas, values, and beliefs about "what it means to be a Woman". Wild Woman is bold, fierce, and, of course, Wild! She creates space to live an authentically creative life. She frees up her life force energy. She is the force in us that wakes us from our habitual sleep to blaze a trail into a new way of being. Change is her way of being - transition, the in-between spaces. She knows destruction, like Kali Ma, burning down illusions with fierce Love. She lights a torch inside of us, and keeps the flame alive, so that we know where to return to when she calls our name. She is of wild reckoning, unashamed in her naked expression, untamed in her devotion to feeling it all.

For this, Wild Woman has been rejected, exiled by the existing wounded male power structure, and hidden away by us Women out of fear of similar treatment for ourselves and our daughters. She represents a part of the female psyche that has been locked in a cage marked with the warning, "Danger: Unacceptable Behaviour!"

Like all wild beings, Wild Woman is always looking for ways to escape her cage, to get out to hunt, roam, and play. Regardless of our paying attention to her howls or growls, she lives in all of us Women, and, just like the wild animal that has been caged, the more we ignore her, the louder and more insistent that she gets.

Wheel of Fulfillment

As Women are receptors, we are magnets for attracting our deepest desires and portals for birthing our creative projects to life, both literally and figuratively. Inner Autumn is the time in our creative cycle when we see the fruits of our endeavours fully ripened, and ready for receiving through the Harvest. This is a potent time for getting in tune with the energy of fulfillment, as it begins to shift inward and downward toward our roots during the transition from Summer to Winter, readying for Harvest. Here in this space, one of great openness and intuition, we can tune into Mama Earth deeply, the energy of receptivity and openness.

The Wheel of Fulfillment exercise shown below invites us to feel into the various areas of our life, and use our intuitive abilities, becoming aware of where we are currently focusing our energy, and where we could lean into different areas for greater wholeness and balance. It can be done anytime; however, we may receive especially deeper insights while we are in our luteal phase leading up to bleeding, or during the Waning Moon.

The way that the Wheel of Fulfillment works is for us to reflect on each of the six areas outlined below, and to give some honest thought and feeling about how fulfilled we feel in this area of our lives. There are many areas in life where we Women can place our energy, and those shown are just six that cover the common areas of our lives. These can be divided into more sections of course; the invitation is for us to have fun with it, and to make it our own. If we are feeling unfulfilled or stuck in a particular area of our life, we can notice what matters most, and choose to align our energy differently, taking action as needed. There are Reflection questions below the Wheel that can be done at some point after completing the Wheel.

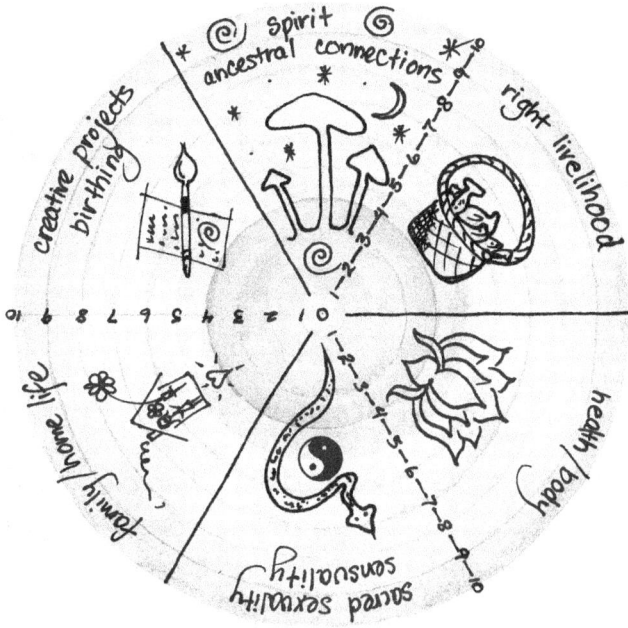

Reflections

- In what area of your life do you feel *most* fulfilled? Why?

- What is an awareness that has come through when you look at your *Wheel of Fulfillment*?

- In what area do you feel the *least* fulfilled? Why?

- Is there any area that you feel that you are blocking yourself from receiving?

- How can you better create the space for deeper fulfillment?

- What is the one thing that, if it didn't happen, you would feel unfilled in life? What can you do to create space for this to happen?

The Downward Descent

In March, 2020, I had just finished guiding a 10-day Embodiment & Meditation Retreat in Costa Rica through The Peace Room, a meditation studio that I had co-created with a couple of friends. We had been secluded blissfully in the beautiful jungles and mountains of Costa Rica where we spent our days connecting with our natural surroundings and coming together in circle for meditation and embodiment practices.

In the airport, I noticed so many people wearing masks and wasn't sure what was going on. The TV screens were talking about a virus and a global pandemic. Concerned and confused, we flew back to our city, and it was there that one of my business partners filled us in on what had been going on while we had been contentedly tucked away in the lushness of Costa Rica. Everything went into lockdown a few days later.

The studio had to be closed, and the business and community that we had worked for three years to help birth into life was put on hold. Like so many others, I had no idea of what was to come - for myself, my family, my livelihood, or my community.

Like many other studios, we transitioned as best as we could to online classes and other offerings to our clients to stay afloat, but so much income was lost with the doors closed. Downtown Ottawa looked apocalyptic, with a large amount of offices closed, and employees working from home. The fate of the business was looking dismal at this point, and my partners and I wondered how much longer we could survive, if this continued to go on. After just a few weeks of lockdown, I had a feeling that things were not as they seemed.

Weeks turned into months, and as the plans for re-opening the economy became public knowledge, it became more discouraging to imagine a future where the studio could do well. When we heard about the "regulations" for re-opening, we wondered how that could possibly work; the regulations went against everything that The Peace Room was built on, completely out of alignment with the values of the business. We realized that we could not survive without regular clients supporting the business, so we finally decided to leave the physical location closed permanently. We had no choice but to let things die, and then grieve what had been lost.

In the summer of 2020, many people I knew were questioning what was going on; news of groups of protestors on Vancouver Island, British Columbia, reached us. The idea of selling everything and leaving to go to the West Coast in trailers was brought up, and it became a regular topic of con-

versation. The idea awoke a passion in me - the same deep level of passion that I had felt years back, when the Wild Woman had howled loudly to me, and I then left my first marriage.

While holding this passion in my heart, I was also overcome with an immense feeling of guilt and grief, as I faced the reality of having to leave my older children behind. How was I going to be able to do what my children wanted me to do - and what others expected me to do, while also doing what I felt was exactly what I needed to do to join others in community at this important time in modern history?

As I witnessed family after family preparing to go west, I couldn't deny the pull to join them. Logically, I rationalized that my children would be okay staying with their father while I was away, and that I wasn't planning to be gone forever. But still, no amount of rationalizing could possibly have prepared me for the consequences of the decision that I made to leave.

Luke and I spent the next two months selling all that we owned, save for the few things we could fit in our newly acquired 5th wheel trailer. On a rainy Autumn day, we left Ottawa and headed for Vancouver Island, our 200 sq. ft home in tow, leaving behind my 17-year-old daughter and my 13-year-old son with their father.

The journey west was full of immense challenges that felt like parts of me were being called upon for a great initiation. I felt like I couldn't keep my head above water, as if wave after *wave was pulling me under the surface, unable to catch my breath.*

We had challenges with the trailer and the truck beyond what we had ever thought would happen. A tire fell off while driving on the highway and rolled across the road; a window fell out, and we still have no idea where it went; we got stuck in Manitoba for days waiting for trailer parts so that we could resume traveling, and were told that, given the state of the world, they could take months to arrive.

Meanwhile, our savings account was emptying quickly. We were unsure of how we'd be able to make ends meet on our small income once we got out west, or if we'd even make it there at all. I began to question everything, including the reasons for leaving in the first place, feeling somehow I was being punished, old programs and beliefs running on repeat in my mind, telling me that I was a crazy, selfish mother for making this decision.

The trailer got repaired and we were back on the road again, headed West to meet the other families who had left before us.

A message came through one day while driving through the prairies, an intervention. I had chosen to listen to an audiobook Clarissa Pinkola Estes' Women Who Run With the Wolves. In one of her stories, Estes speaks about a mother's choice to leave when she hears the Wild Calling of her heart. Tears streaming down my face, I knew that she was speaking of me, to me. I was the Wild Woman that she was talking about, and the Wild Woman was in me, working through me, calling me west.

At the same time, the pain in my heart for my children was so immense, I felt like my chest was going to explode. Grief, despair, guilt, and shame were flooding my energy field, and welled up in my throat and spilled from my eyes.

As I sobbed, while trying to keep my eyes on the road, I looked in the rearview mirror and something caught my eye - an image that I had seen every day since we had left Ottawa, but that I had never fully taken notice of before this moment.

On the front of the fifth wheel trailer was a large image of three wolves - one mama and two cubs. There was no doubt that this image was of me and my two older kids.

Something deep in my being shifted, a validation that I was doing the right thing by following my Inner Wild calling, that I was exactly where I was meant to be.

Yet, I wondered if my daughter and son would ever come to understand that I had made the decision to leave to create a better life for my whole family - for them, for all of us- and if they would forgive me. I trusted that they would see the truth in it all one day.

I cannot say in all honesty that the message from Estes, and the vision of the wolf mother and her cubs made everything better from then on; the pain of separation, and the *guilt over my actions, were cutting deeply, and, at that point, I still had a long way to travel, outwardly and inwardly, to ultimately get to where I knew I wanted to be.*

After two weeks of seemingly endless trial, we finally arrived on Van Isle. By then, the other families were already there settling in, and the overall vibe in the community was one of new adventure and celebration.

I found myself feeling apart from it all. Now, with my feet settled upon firm rock sticking out of the Pacific Ocean, I found myself sinking back down into my own world of guilt, grief, and worry, and my heart feeling like it was being pulled out of my chest, 5000 kms away, back to Ottawa.

The months to come would be filled with more initiations into my Wild Woman, while living beside the shrouded Pacific Ocean, among the ancient, mossy, dense forests, which seemed to be orchestrating many deep dives into my Shadow, and the transformation of the Woman whom I had been up to that point. Death of the old was beckoning, and I was led into the deep dark abyss of my own becoming.

Anger & Rage

At some point in the initiation phase of our Wild Woman, we will likely meet both Anger and Rage head-on. For us Women, these two emotions, just like the Wild Woman herself, have been caged, locked away.

Women have been taught that it's not alright to openly express anger. There can be so much shame surrounding Women's expression of anger, as we are told that it is neither feminine nor attractive. Because of what we may have seen and learned growing up, both in our families and the over-culture, we often keep our anger hidden, usually for a long time, out of a deep-seated fear that, if we were to let it out and allow others to witness it in us, we will neither be loved nor loveable, accepted nor acceptable, respected nor re-spectable.

In the male-valued over-culture, an angry Woman is char-acterized as "crazy", as a "bitch" or both. Quite to the con-trary, for Men, Anger and Rage are not only expected, but revered and respected.

As "good girls", "good wives", and "good mothers", we Women have done our best to conform with societal expec-tations, which require that we suppress our indignation, hurt, anger, and rage - both in ourselves and in our daugh-ters, creating the next generation of "good girls".

Not surprisingly, Women often carry around a lot of anger. Often, we feel angry because we haven't been per-mitted to express our feelings about how we have been treated by another; a feeling of powerlessness overcomes us, and this burns inside, because it needs to come out.

Anger initially shows up when a boundary has been crossed (known or unknown), when it feels like a button has been pushed, when there's a burning feeling that some-thing has gone against our will and our natural way of being.

We have a choice at this point - to react by saying or do-ing something, or to say or do nothing. Our socially condi-tioned response might lead us to choose to just sit with it, because reacting in the moment, when we feel the anger arise, often does not feel like the right thing to do.

However, sitting with it doesn't necessarily dissipate the energy that has boiled up in us, nor allow for healing. All too often, the anger gets ignored or buried deep inside, creat-ing a disruption or blockage in the flow of our energy, po-tentially leaking out later in some other seemingly unrelated set of circumstances.

When left unexpressed, anger stays in our energy field, and becomes repressed. This anger energy still needs a pathway to move through the body, so, failing this, it may show up as something else - an illness, a life crisis, a wakeup call.

The truth is, Anger needs to be expressed in some form. If it is not, over time, unexpressed Anger becomes rage, in-dividually and collectively. Rage resides in the roots, deep deep, down. It is a completely wild expression, without care of what it looks like or sounds like, frothing at the mouth, fangs exposed, ready to strike.

The Wild Woman, who has been caged for years, even decades, cannot be expected to be nice when we let her loose. She may be ready to devour anything in her path, fangs dripping with saliva, thirsting for blood! She may lash out without being aware of where the venom inside of her is coming from. Re-awakening any unresolved trauma from her youth, she may not care about the pain of others. She may become violent, ready to rip into others as a result of being pushed back and kept hidden for so long.

Rage is the primal energy that shows up when boundaries have been deeply violated - individually and on a mass scale. It is especially connected to our ancestral healing. As Women, we experience rage collectively when we feel into the devastation of how Women around the world, for the past few thousand years, have been mistreated, sold, held back, punished, tortured, raped, mutilated, and oppressed - simply and only because they were born with vulvas and wombs. We feel this collective rage when we think of children being mistreated and abused, and of our Earth Mother, The Great Mother, being raped and taken from without permission or gratitude. We feel this when we, too, have been violated.

The denial and suppression of our Anger and Rage keep us from our deepest sense of freedom - and even our Pleasure. It is through feeling and emoting them that we find the keys to the doors where healing and wholeness reside. If we are ready to take a look inside, there are many gifts that they can offer us.

What do Anger and Rage have to teach us? What are their medicines?

Anger shows us where we have given too much out of feeling obligated or pressured, and where we have not honoured our own personal boundaries. Welcoming it and thanking it for letting us know when we are not being respected often opens us to a new way of being in our lives; we set healthier boundaries and honour ourselves in new ways that feel supportive and nutritive.

Anger is restless energy and needs space to breathe, and to move. It is often a catalyst for change, the kind of energy that spurs us into action - cutting things loose, tearing things down, letting things die, speaking our truth – where we couldn't act before.

Because rage is such a deep visceral feeling, it has a profound way of showing us our boundaries: It is an honouring of our sacred NO, which leads to our sacred YES. When we are clearer on our boundaries and lovingly uphold them, we spend less of our creative life force energy on others and this creates space for awakening our passions and gifts, a part of us that is here to offer a new way forward. Rage offers an opening to deeper freedom and Joy, an expansiveness into a new realm of possibility. Our Inner Child receives our Love and recognition, we step into the role of Protectress, and fiercely defend what is most innocent and pure about us and the world we live in. Rage helps us to avoid bypassing our feelings and pay attention to our instincts, knowing that they have a place and are here to guide us through.

The process of integrating our Anger and Rage is a sacred passageway, and they need to be attended to with reverence. When we create space for Anger and Rage to be fully seen and welcomed, we can bring them out of the shadows, and integrate them into our wholeness. They then cease to unconsciously control us, and we can then see their beauty as the gifts they truly are, here to teach us.

The Gifts of Grief

I had left my two children. I had left them behind to live in a trailer on Vancouver Island. Five-thousand kilometers of forests, scrub, rock, lakes, plains, hills, mountains, valleys, badlands, desert, rivers, and the Salish Sea now lay between us. The shocking reality of this cold fact pulled me down into a depth of grief that I had never felt before. I missed them both so much that I felt like parts of me had been ripped out, torn off. The only thing that seemed to be keeping me breathing and going forward was that they would be coming out for the December holidays.

On many of the rainy days, I would find myself walking along the ocean's edge, looking out in the distance, knowing that I could just walk in and never come back. Or I would be standing at the edge of a cliff, looking down, knowing all it took was just a few more steps, and the pain would be all over. The immensity and weight of the pain felt like it was just too much for me to carry, like it was going to explode on its own, if I didn't put an end to it all soon. I felt numb to the outside world, engulfed in the darkness of my inner storms, unable to feel Joy, like I had before. Feelings of immense failure overcame me at every turn. I felt like I couldn't catch my breath, from the waves of grief forcing me down into the depths over and over again, unable to make my way up to the surface to catch a glimpse of the sun on my face for longer than what seemed like a brief moment.

Still, I knew that there was no going back, not right then. Vancouver Island is a temperate rainforest, rarely experiencing snow or frigid temperature. Its climate is what had allowed us to be able to live in the trailer all winter. Back in Ottawa, we could not have survived the bitter-cold winter temperatures in the trailer. There was not enough money to rent an apartment, and we had sold everything we owned anyway. The studio and community that my partners and I had birthed into existence no longer existed. And our family and many of our friends were now far out of reach for a hug.

This wasn't the first time that I had encountered grief. There had certainly been other times when the pain of grief was so thick and unmoving, that it had been a challenge to see myself through to the other side.

Akaiy'ha

During my separation and divorce from my children's father years earlier, the pain of that process was so unbearable, that I remember, on multiple occasions, having the thought that I could drive my car into the post on the side of the highway, that I could end this pain right then and there. And then, right after this, I would picture my children's faces, and tears would stream down my face, my heart ready to burst from my chest, knowing that I would be taking something from them that they needed - a mother to care for them and to love them, a mother for them to love. For their sake, I couldn't bring myself to do it. I kept on driving.

But this time, walking through the ghostly forests and the damp mists of ocean spray, the call to end it all felt different. I had left my children behind. My connection to them felt like it was being stretched thin. Did they even need me anymore?

The pain of being separated from all that I knew and loved was vast and deep, much like the ocean that was crashing relentlessly nearby; grief was its own kind of wild.

Soon, though, I began to notice how the ocean was showing me my inner world, noticing the grief inside and the ocean outside; eventually, they became one. On days when the sun shone (this isn't very often on the island in the winter), the ocean was calm, the birds came out, the eagles soared high, and my spirits were like the eagles - lifted. On days it was rainy and windy, I would cry from the pain; the dark gloom seemed like it would split me in two.

One day, I received word that my children would not be allowed by their father to come to visit over the December holidays. It felt like that pivotal moment in the car all those years ago.

Rage was welling up in me, and I left the confines of the trailer. It was a stormy day, and the wind was howling. I ran to the ocean, and picked up a large rock and screamed, "FUU-UUUCCCCKKKK YYYOOOOOUUUU!!!" , and hurled the rock into the water. Fueled further by the rage, I picked up yet more rocks and pelted them into the ocean, screaming and swearing at the top of my lungs.

I didn't care who might be watching from their little trailer windows. I imagined I may have already been known as "that crazy lady", the one who spends hours outside talking to herself, picking up seashells, and staring out into the ocean. None of this mattered.

I continued yelling and screaming, and throwing anything that I could lift out into the waves, until I felt like I needed to move, quickly. Following what was arising in my body and trusting the process of this deep excavation, I headed to the trail that led to the forest, running on the path at the edge of the ocean in my rubber boots, being pummeled by the driving rain, soaked to the bone. Crying. Running. The pain inside of me now seemed beyond bearable.

And then it came to me that it was about more than this one instance. I had ripped open a part of my heart that hadn't been touched in a while, that had been hidden for so long. I was feeling anger and rage rushing to the surface from other events in my life. I was angry and enraged at my parents for the things that I experienced when growing up that no child should. I was feeling anger and rage at my kids' father for not allowing them to travel and see me. And I was angry and enraged at myself for choosing to leave - I was so incredibly angry at myself. The wild ocean was calling all of this forth from me, and I was being asked to surrender to it yet again, to let it move through.

After running and letting the tears flow for what seemed like forever, the energy of my anger and rage had diminished, and I had begun to slow down. Reaching a turning point at the edge of the forest on the path, I stopped. Breathing heavily, I stood still for a few minutes, taking in the wisdom of the ocean, and then turned around to head back to the trailer, walking this time.

Today wouldn't be the day my life ended, but the grief of not having my older children with me, felt so unbearable, there was a part of me that had wished differently.

A week later, I traveled to Ucluelet to spend a week in a cabin alone for my 40th birthday. I needed the space to heal what had been coming up for me, to let go and let things die, to listen. I had never spent that amount of time alone, and the gift of taking the space to grieve the loss of so much felt really important for me.

Luke, who had been so incredibly supportive and loving

while navigating his own challenges and transformation, along with my youngest little one who brought so much play and Joy into my life, were beacons through many of the storms, guiding me back home. But this time, I felt I needed to rely on something from within, to find my way through it, I could feel something coming through that I needed to be alone for.

There were no distractions, and I wanted it that way. During that week, there were baths - a lot of baths - walks on the Wild Pacific Trail, and the medicine of grief. The trail walks were journeys, each one showing me something I needed to see, messages from the Great Mother.

One day, during a walk in a storm that nobody was fit to be out in, the universe sent me a sign. There were only three other people on that trail - a mother and her two grown children. We were all soaking wet from the storm, and she asked me to take a picture of them. She told me that they were visiting from out of town, that she lived there, and they didn't. My heart felt a deep yearning for my own children to be there, a sense of emptiness flooding my heart and womb.

Soaked to the bone, I went back to the cabin and took quite possibly the longest bath of my life. I cried and mourned all that I had thought my life would be. Grief was my teacher. When the pain became too unbearable, I would surrender deeper into it, allowing it to engulf me, to enclose me in its darkness, to sink into the death of it all. I recalled the gifts that the Magickal Mycelium had given to me through many journeys with them - learning to surrender, to let the medicine do its work, to allow things to shift without interfering, struggling, or fighting against the flow.

Tears continued to pour out of my eyes, into the bath water; the depth of pain was endless it seemed. Eventually, I felt emptied, like I had cried all of the tears out of my body. But the pain of letting go had opened something up; an opening in the internal chambers of my heart and soul gave birth to a power in me that had been asleep for so long.

At some point in that tub on that fateful day, my focus turned to the sensations of my body. I became so aware of the water, the temperature, my breath, my skin. The grief was transforming, and I was witnessing. Immense waves of pleasure rippled through my being - wet, aroused, alive. I was being baptized in the sacredness of my divine and sacred sensuality, innocently and wildly attentive to each pulsation, and embodying both my Masculine and Feminine, watching the dance of Love commence with me. I lost track of time, the curves of my body taking me to far off places, deserts, oceans, mountains, and rivers, meeting the Goddess through the landscape of my being.

I arose from the tub, dripping with arousal and intrigue, seeing the reflection of myself in the mirror, now smiling back at me. I walked to the bedroom, and I began to set the room as if an important sexy guest was about to arrive, placing candles and crystals, turning down the lights, and placing a bottle of oil on the bedside table. I burned some medicine to cleanse the room. A ceremony of Self Love was about to begin. Every detail felt like it mattered; this was for me and me alone. I put some music on, and danced naked around the room, shaking and moving my body every which way, loving every second of pure, ecstatic bliss.

Eventually, I lay down on the bed and breathed deeply for a few moments, allowing my body to settle into the rhythm of the moment. I let my hands glide over my body, feeling every curve, loving every part. It was another initiation, one that led me to the temple of my Inner Priestess, her magick and mystery waiting there for me all along. I felt like Inanna, descending into the Underworld through The Seven Gates, letting go at each threshold, naked and empty, and then full and alive. My hands were the lover of my Inner Masculine, touching my body in ways that made my Inner Feminine cry with Pleasure. It was soft and sweet, hard and pulsating, a wondrous exploration into the vast cosmos of my innermost world. I let it all out, any remnants of grief, tears, sadness, anger, rage, heartache, unworthiness, through the channel of pure bliss and ecstatic union. I became a puddle on the bed, deeply relaxed, fulfilled, grinning from ear to ear. I went to sleep with the sound of the storm still raging outside; a storm nobody was fit to be out in, except for the wild souls who needed to find their way through the storm back home.

I woke the next morning, feeling restored, and with a sense of fullness alive in me.

Reflecting on the previous evening, I thought, it wasn't the first time I made love to myself, but it felt like I had touched into a new depth - a softness that had been covered up by something hard, a protection, a shell.

Grief had given me an immense gift - Pleasure.

Oozing, soft, mushy, slippering, tingling, steamy, hot, drippy, PLEASURE-filled wonder.

As I had surrendered and softened to grief, I had opened channels in myself that gave birth to Pleasure in ways beyond what I could have accessed without it. This brought back immense JOY into my life, like a beacon guiding me home when lost in a storm.

Bath

All of the times when I felt so alone
You were there for me
Reminding me of my ability to shift and change
To become hot or cold at the turn of a knob

To settle in for a nice dip

You were inside
Outside
Everywhere

You soothed the hurt out
With your gentle touch
Nothing ever seems so bad
In the bath

Reclaiming Sexual Sovereignty & Restoring Wholeness

Opening the Gateway to the Lower Body ~ The Throat-Heart-Womb-Pussy Connection

The stories and imprints of our past experiences arise when we go into the deepest parts of ourselves, and these offer us the keys to healing and restoring Wholeness, to Reclaiming our Sovereign Self as our Birthright.

As women, with bodies that are largely Receptors and Channels when it comes to Birthing and Sex, our Wombs and Yonis hold the Energetic Imprints of all past experiences. Where we have felt open to Life and receptive, we open further, leaning into the experience of Life in each moment.

As we have seen in this book so far, there is a connection between Grief and Pleasure, and between Pain and Personal Power. When we speak of Personal Power, it is not the kind of power that takes over and tries to control, oppress, suppress, coerce, or enslave – "Power *Over*". NO. This is not *True* Power, but instead, a *distortion* of what is True. True Power is the Power of Love, the Ineffable Force that created us all with the greatest hopes and visions for all of Humanity. And True Power is our Sacred Right, as is our Pleasure, to move through life without Trauma.

Why do we still live in a world where people, particularly children, are being physically, emotionally, mentally, and sexually abused and raped?

Trauma. Deeply rooted trauma.

We have lost our way, strayed too far from the Wisdom of what is Good about Humanity, and we have forgotten to protect the Innocence of Life itself, of the Children, and all Life on Earth.

Why?

For several thousand years, humankind has been traumatized by living in a world where Fear, Violence, War,

Greed, Rape, and Conquer has been prioritized. Generally and individually, directly or indirectly, none of us have been left unscathed, to one degree or another. And we haven't taken the necessary paths to healing together.

When we are sexually abused as a child, there certainly is Trauma to our body at the time of the abuse. Or later in our life, when we may experience trauma to our Sexual Nervous System through being treated as a product in over-medicalized systems, and through invasive procedures that do not support and encourage our body's self healing abilities . But what does our body do with this Trauma? What happens to us when our Temple has been violated?

We close off, shut down, and erect walls around our Hearts, Wombs, and Yonis. We learn to distrust others, and we learn to doubt that life is really meant to be Joyful and Pleasurable. We accept Pain as our natural state of being, and we learn to live in the head, on the front step to our only True Homes – that of our Bodies.

We become disconnected due to unhealthy Roots to ground and sustain us; our Throats close down, unable to fully or even partly express the pain of what has happened, or of what continues to happen within us on "repeat" - years and decades later.

If the Sacred Passageway of our Yonis, leading to the temple of our Wombs, is entered without our Permission, without our Informed Consent, without our Full Body YES, we retreat within ourselves. We lock a part of ourselves, our

Joy and our Pleasure away, deep within the Womb Space.

The issues that settle into the tissues arise later in life as a cry for help from our Inner Child, our younger self who had endured unwanted, possibly violent, entry, who had been without the power or experience to fully defend our boundaries, and certainly without any experience or voice around our likes or dislikes.

When Sexual Trauma is present....

- We may distrust women and carry a Sister Wound or Mother Wound if we feel that we should have been protected by the Women in our lives.
- We may play a provocative role to get attention, or we may manipulate our bodies to fit the over-culture's pornographic model.
- We may give away free admission to the Sacred Temple of our bodies to those who do not deserve entry, because there is a voice that is not ours telling us that we are broken, shameful, and unworthy of Wholeness.
- We may disassociate and disconnect from our own bodies.
- We may shut down sexually and be unable to experience other sensual pleasures.
- We may become numb and avoidant emotionally, while we wear a hard shell, feeling only a sense of emptiness.
- We may lack a sense of belonging, of being able to feel "at home" in the world, but rather like a detached outside observer looking in on Life.
- We may feel like we don't even know ourselves, and we

are not comfortable in our own skins.

- We may experience anxiety, fear, depression, panic attacks, flashbacks, obsessions, hyper-alertness, difficulty sleeping, irritability, anger.
- We may feel a sense of unknown yearning, like something has been lost.
- We may be without enough energy to get through our days, or we may be restless, unable to settle, and always busy.
- We may disguise harmful behaviours, including alcohol and drug abuse, and overspending, as just having fun, or as "Wild", when it is actually arising as a call for help.
- We may have disordered thinking around food.
- We may think about or do harm to ourselves and others.
- We may have difficulty establishing stable relationships because of the resulting issues around abandonment, betrayal, helplessness, submission.
- We may have difficulty functioning as Mothers to our children, with our instincts cut off from the Motherboard of our Sacred Womb and Heart Connection.
- We may develop an illness in our Breasts or Wombs, or a disharmony in the tissues of our Pussies.

Where we have been violated, that is, where our own personal boundary has been crossed – whether we were or were not aware at the time - we close down, folding our petals to the Sun and retreating deeply back into our roots for safety.

Additionally, in Generational Trauma, patterns of Abuse and Trauma are passed down through the generations.

With Oppressive Colonial Structures having been forced upon our Ancestors, these still wield their "Power Over" us today, since it may feel like there are not deep enough roots to nourish us and to support us through to the other side of healing. If it was Generational Sexual Trauma that had been perpetrated, this creates further imprinting in the tissues of our Womb Space, Heart, Throat, and Pussy.

We hold onto traumatic memories in our bodies, until we feel safe to fully process what has transpired, and move through the healing process, back to Wholeness, reclaiming our Sovereign Sexual Power once again, reclaiming our Voice.

If abuse has occurred in our past, and especially if we were children at the time it occurred, we learn to close ourselves off in various ways, we may learn to protect what tenderness and innocence remains and put up a shield to whoever may come too close, even if they have good intentions and would never intentionally cause harm to us.

When abuse occurs during childhood, and especially as we are approaching the onset of menstruation, it has a major impact on our sexual development. It has been reported that 90% of sexual abuse and molestation happens with someone that is known and trusted by the victim. I use the word "victim" very seldom anymore, but, here, "victim" is appropriately used.

Who is the Protectress of the Innocent in a world that goes on consuming itself into extinction, while harming the

Earth and all her inhabitants?

The Dark Feminine.

She lives in each of us, in ALL OF US.

The Dark Feminine is Mother Earth embodied, she goes by many names and lives in the darker parts of the Moon cycle and our personal cycle. She is the energy that birthed the Dark Goddesses that were hidden away and the Archetypes of Wild Woman, Wise Woman, Witch, Priestess, and Medicine Woman.

She is the bridge between the Old and New, who is blazing a torch into the darkest caves of our Collective Consciousness.

She is the one who breaks us free from the chains of human opinion and dares to claim herself Sovereign and Free.

She carries the Wisdom of the Old Ways, a time when Life was Sacred, and Children were protected by both Women and Men in their families and communities.

She is the answer we have been waiting for.

She is here to awaken the planet NOW, to help us reclaim what was lost, and to restore Wholeness to ourselves and our Earth Home.

There is a process we must go through, one of Reclamation and Restoration to Wholeness. It is partly a solo journey, and partly a shared one with those who we invite in - our Sexual Partners, our Families, and a Community of Women and Men with whom we walk this journey.

When we first embark on this journey, we will most certainly rub up against any old wounds that are present. We may stumble to find our way in the Wild, outside of the oppressive over-culture and its systems, and, as we make our way there, it may not look pretty, or pleasant. In fact, it will not resemble any part of our journey up to that point.

From the outside, it may look to others like we are unraveling at the seams, burning bridges, or going on a wild ravenous rampage, seemingly for attention. Yes, it may look like this at first. But, at some point, we will find ourselves standing at the entrance to the Temple doors to our Sacred Wholly Ground, with the Goddess ready to welcome us Home once again.

And when we do...

We may fall to our knees and weep, opening up the floodgates for Grief to pour through.
We may weep for our Inner Wild Child, and what we could have been or become, if the abuse had not happened.
We may weep for all of the times we allowed someone to touch us, or enter our Sacred Temple, without a full *YES* from our body.
We may meet Anger and Rage, and wear them as badges of honour for a while, because, subconsciously, we need the

Pain to be seen.
We may feel fearful of the changes we must make, and what is to come in the vast, unknowable landscape of our life going forward.

And, at some point we must make a choice.

Will we choose a life of Joy and Pleasure, or one of Pain and Disconnect?

How can we possibly find our way back Home, back to Wholeness?

Through deep listening, and re-entering the Gates to our Sacred Remembrance, on our own Terms, coming back to our Cyclical Ways as Women, held in the memory of our blood and bones, and integrating this Wisdom back into our daily lives through Ceremony and Ritual. There is a pathway that is laid throughout this book, in the Cyclical Wisdom pieces, through story, poetry, and practices. This pathway is an opening, an invitation to go deeper into the body and discover the treasure that awaits us, even if it has been covered up or buried. When Trauma has come into our lives and made us hide ourselves or hold ourselves in patterns that keep us stuck, it is within our Power to reclaim what we feel has been lost, and we can do this by restoring ourselves to Wholeness through following nature's way, through getting in touch with our Wombs and Yonis and remembering that we are perfect, just like every part of nature; that we are not broken, we are all Goddesses Embodied.

Sexual Nervous System and the Cervix

Our Wombs and Yonis are abundant forests of interaction with the world, both around us and within us. There are more nerves in our Sexual Organs than any other area of our bodies. The collective complex of our Central Nervous System that emanates from our Womb Space - our Uterus, Fallopian Tubes, Ovaries, and Cervix, and nerve connections as well as energetic imprints of these where they have been removed - and includes the Sacred Space of our Yonis - Clitoris, Vulva, Labia, Venus Monds, Bladder, Urethral Sponge, Vaginal Canal and opening - as well as our Anus and Rectum, is what I call the *Sexual Nervous System*. The nerves in this system are like roots reaching out to every cell, like antennae in our Energetic Auric Field – and much like the Magickal Mycelium that grow below and over the Forest floor - connecting every part of the experience in each moment.

The nerves in our sexual organs form a powerful superhighway of information beginning at the lower part of our body and energy centers, cycling up to the upper energy centers and back down again, and through the macrocosmic orbit of our natural breath cycle. Our Sexual Nervous System emanates from the Womb and Pussy outward, where we can tap into our deepest Pleasure and Life Force Energy, and where we must venture into for Wholeness and Reclamation, when Trauma is held in the tissues.

The Throat is a gateway into the body and out, as are the Cervix and Yoni; they are intimately and deeply connected in our Feminine Vessel. The Cervix is a gateway through which life is birthed and symbolic death occurs. It is a Portal to the Moon inside of us that keeps time with the rhythms of the Goddess herself. The Cervix - when touched, massaged, and stimulated through deep diaphragmatic breath, emits DMT (Dimethyltryptamine), also known as the "God Molecule", or in this case, "The Goddess Molecule!" Massive amounts of Pleasure Hormones are sent out like waves through the body when we tap into the treasure held in the Cervix.

Because of the Cervix being an extreme pleasure center, Birthing can be an Orgasmic process. As the baby's head and body move from the inner world of the Womb, through the doorway of the Cervix, the high concentration nerves are stimulated.

It is the energy in these roots that are the foundation for the birthing experience. If our body is holding onto imprint patterns from earlier Trauma to our Wombs, Cervix, or Yoni, our roots cannot be healthy, and we cannot bloom fully. We will not be fully open to the Pleasure that the birthing experience can offer us. We may resist the flow of the current, holding onto the edges, kicking and screaming, unable to Let Go and Surrender, unable to float and let the current guide us gently through. If we bite down on the Pain, and just endure it, instead of releasing it and setting ourselves free, we limit, or even close off, the current of easeful Birth and Transformation.

The Cervix is the Passageway of our Sacred Psychedelic Birthright, the Gateway to tapping into ocean-deep waves of Ecstasy and Grounded Presence. This same Gateway, is also part of an important connection, the Vagus Nerve Connection, linking the upper and lower Energy Centres. This connection, linking our Throat, Heart, Womb, and Yoni, holds memories that have been accumulated since our Birth into the Earth Realm, and provides a passageway for Healing and Restoration, when needed. The Vagus Nerve can be stimulated through Touch, Breath, and Sound, sending a reverberation through nerves in and around the spinal column down to the lower body, releasing patterns of stress and tension being held there.

When the Cervix is tight and holding, our jaw, too, can be tight or in pain, and vice versa. However, when we open our mouths to Sound, Chant or Sing, in a way that invites Pleasure in, we send vibrations that invite opening and release, down the spine through the Vagus Nerve system, to the roots at the base, opening up our ability to feel into a deeper experience of Orgasmic Pleasure and Presence.

In each of us, there exists the Power to Heal and come back to Wholeness, despite whatever has happened in our past, whatever things have stayed with us from childhood, whatever is keeping us stuck and in an energy of feeling unloved or unaccepted, or whatever pieces of ourselves that we feel have been missing.

The beauty about our bodies and their ability to heal comes full circle when we realize that there is nothing we cannot heal from, that there is nothing that has been taken that cannot be restored in some way. We can Heal from the past and we can begin again, with a renewed sense of Vitality and Purpose. The Moon with her cycles shows us how Healing and Wholeness come from moving through the Seasons of Life, and that, after each Winter, there is always a Spring and New Life.

The journey of Reclaiming our Sexual Sovereignty begins with each of us, once we feel ready to embrace all of the gifts that await us.

Some of us may microdose our way through the healing, and some of us may feel we need to take a more intense approach. Whatever the approach is that we choose, we should choose wisely. This means not giving ourselves too much to hold, and providing our nervous systems with the space needed, both beforehand to prepare for the experience, and afterward to integrate it, reflect on what has left, and feel into what has been created through the process.

Reflecting and resting, making time for ourselves, and adjusting our lifestyles to encompass healthy behaviours that will help us to feel supported from within, as well as the support from others, when needed - are all vital to our well-being as we integrate healing experiences.

A major part of Sexual Sovereign Reclamation is taking responsibility for our healing, and recognizing where we may need support or help, while also owning what is ours to heal. When we work with others, whether through one-to-one support, or group energy, it is important to have trust-worthy and trusting relations with those who we allow along on our journey. If we are feeling anxious or confused during the process, or uncertain of the next steps, using our voice to express how we are feeling, and what we need to con-tinue, is not only important, but vitally necessary, if we are to Heal and move forward on our journey, with ease and a lightness in our Spirit. There are times when we may require Solitude and other times when a Community of others to support us, through witnessing and listening, can help us to find our way back to Wholeness - that space where there is nothing to fix or mend, where we are perfect as we are, scars and all. Our Reclamation then becomes a Celebration and an opening to creating the life that is our Sacred Birthright, one that invites in deeper Pleasure and Joy.

Humming/ Vagal Toning Practice

Humming and Sounding, done as we exhale, signals to the body that we are safe, at ease, and relaxed. Find a space that feels supportive to do this practice. It is a practice for opening up the channels between the Throat and Pussy, providing also clearing for the Heart and Womb. You may wish to play some music and set up your space for this Self Ceremony in a way that invites in Pleasure, Curiosity, and Support. This could look like gathering cushions and soft throw blankets and placing them in a Nest where you will lie or sit.

- Take 15-20 mins to lie down in the space that you've created for this Self Ceremony.
- Begin by taking deep breaths into the lower belly and womb space, expanding in all directions.
- Continue for several minutes, until you are feeling grounded and supported.
- As you Inhale, send the Breath to your Heart Space and Womb Space, expanding outward.
- As you Exhale, relax your jaw, and open your mouth, saying HAAAAAAAAAAA - letting all of the sound out with the breath.
- Repeat the sound HAAAAAAAAAAA and then allow the sound to change and shift, opening your mouth in various shapes, and giving space for sounds of any kind to come through, without judgment.
- Settle into a natural easy breath for a few minutes.
- Play with the Vowel Sounds, AAAAAA, EEEEEEEEE,

OOOOOOOOO, IIIIIIIIIIII, UUUUUUUU, and allow the sounds to shift and change.
- Place your hands on your Womb Space and send the Sounds down your spine, from your Throat to your Womb and Pussy, allowing opening and softening of the tissues.
- Continue to Sound and Vocalize as it arises; there is no right or wrong way to do this remember. Your unique sound is perfect for you and your body.
- When you feel complete with the Sounding, rest and breathe. Allow the practice to integrate.
- Take notice of how you're feeling after the practice and write down any reflections in your journal.

Note that you may wish to add in movement or massage of Breast, Womb, and Yoni areas, if you're feeling called.

Primal Pussy Reclamation Practice

Do this practice when you have space and time for yourself to go deeper. It is not something that should be rushed, in fact, take all "shoulds" out of it. It is an invitation, as with all practices in this book, and it is vital that you listen to your body as you go through it, and especially tuning into if and when it feels right to even do it. This practice is for YOU and NOBODY ELSE. It is a step in the process of womb and pussy reclamation that I have gone through to reclaim my body for my own Pleasure; you may get a lot from it or a little, either way, it can be empowering if you allow it to be uniquely yours. This practice is to help you get out of the head, where we can live and stay if we have Trauma to the lower body and especially, the Sexual Nervous System, and reside more fully in your own body, taking up the space you need to create the life you desire.

If our bodies feel like they are restricting energy flow, closing, tightening, holding in, or leaking, having poor boundaries, and experiencing any form of dis-ease, this practice offers support for healing and Wholeness.

Make sure you are not going to be disturbed, turn off all electronic devices that may interrupt your process, and let others know that you are entering into a Sacred Ceremony with yourself and not to be interrupted. This in itself, can be a powerful way to uphold a loving boundary, and receive support during the healing process.

There will be an invitation to put your fingers inside your pussy and to touch the Cervix, or where the Cervix has been removed medically, to connect with the energetic imprint that remains after the physical Cervix is no longer there. If that invitation doesn't feel right for you, please listen to that inner voice. Maybe it won't feel right at this moment, and you may come back to it anytime, if and when you're feeling ready. I would encourage you to get curious and remain in the energy of curiosity about your own body and Sexual Nervous System, for the practice, as well as letting your Pleasure, that is, what FEELS GOOD to you and your body, lead the way.

This practice is not about getting anything "right", there

is no course or program you need to take, you do not need to know anatomy well. If you know the anatomy of your Womb Space well, that is wonderful! But, it is not a precursor to doing this exercise, making it accessible for all who have a Womb Space. The practice is about staying with the presence of whatever is arising within you and your reaction to it, allowing yourself to be held by the Sacredness of Life and the Earth Mother that gave you life through your own Mother's body, and allowing e-motions to flow, remembering, that what is held within and what was not fully integrated, Trauma, needs a space to be seen and released, with gentleness and Love.

One final note before we begin. It is vital to remember that although this practice has the power to return us to Wholeness, to heal wounds of the past, and to integrate our Sexual Sovereignty into our bodies once again, we will most likely come face to face with the core wounds that have and still do shape our relational experience with the world around us, within us, and with others. Bearing this in mind and creating a space and intention that feels *deeply supportive and nourishing* to your body and spirit, will set the stage for the process to unfold naturally. You may need to do this process several times to experience a feeling of Wholeness, and please remember, there is no goal, for example, reaching orgasm, or feeling something in particular.

Setting Your Intention: Your intention matters greatly. I invite you to sit with your intention for as long as you need to, before making the decision to embark on this sacred inner exploration of your feminine vessel. And to choose an intention that fosters a deeper love and reverence for yourself and your body, that is solely focused on YOU, and your Pleasure, putting aside any pre-existing ideas about what the word "pleasure" might have meant or still means for you.

You will need a comfortable space to lie down on your back, with lots of pillows to support your body, under your knees, and behind your back if you prefer to be in a slightly reclined position (with your head higher than your hips).

Setting the space for Ceremony, with candles, soft lighting, free of electronic devices, music (if you prefer), and smoke cleansing the space with herbs and medicines of your choice, will help to signal to your Nervous System, and particularly your Sexual Nervous System, that you are Safe, Supported, and Loved. Ensure that the room you are doing this in is quiet, or choosing a time of day where this is the case, and that the temperature is warm enough for you to be naked, or partially naked (waist down), or by placing a blanket on top of you (I often prefer a heated blanket, especially in colder climates or seasons).

The Practice

- Lie down on your back and get comfortable.

- Breathe naturally and settle in, allowing your awareness to focus on your inhales and exhales, without changing the flow. Stay here for a few minutes or as long as you need to feel grounded and ready to move onto the next step.

- Place one hand on your heart, and one on your Womb Space, focusing on cycling your breath between these two areas (Heart Womb Connection Breath outlined on page 105 of this book). Stay here until you feel even more deeply grounded than before and are ready to move onto the next step.

- Continue with this breath and allow any sounds to come through. This process is outlined on page 148 in the *Humming/Vagal Toning Practice*.

- Tune into your Intention for this Practice, once again here, before moving further, and asking if it still resonates or if there is something else that you would like to focus on, heal, release, or call into your bodily experience.

- If you feel called, inviting in your Ancestors (both male and female) or Maternal Ancestors only for support, guidance, and Wisdom. You can ask them to surround you in love and protection, and to guide you through the process with ease and loving support, or anything that you wish to say or invite in. (This step, as with all, is completely optional. If it doesn't feel right, don't do it.)

- Next, place one hand on your heart and one of your mons Venus, the fleshy part covering your pubic bone area where the highest concentration of pubic hair usually grows, at the top of your Yoni. You may wish to cup the area with your (warm) hand or hover the hand over the area if cupping the area doesn't feel right for you.

- Cycle your breath between your Yoni and Heart, just as you did with the Heart Womb Connection Breath, but this time, focusing on these two areas and their connection to each other, and to you.

- Stay here for as long as needed. BREATHE, and notice what emotions are arising, letting them be felt and allowing them to flow through without needing to analyze them.

- (This may be where you STOP, and go no further, saving the entering of your Sacred Gardens for another time if that pleases you, you are in complete control.) Check in with yourself and feel into where you're at, taking any time you need to write down reflections that have arisen so far if you're feeling called. If and when you are ready to move onto the next step, proceed with loving awareness, and letting your breath and body guide you deeper.

- Still with one hand on your heart and one on your mons Venus, taking some deeper intentional breaths and sending the breath down the spine to the root, your Yoni. Continue with doing this breath (or any form of breath that invites deeper relaxation for you), for a few minutes longer, until you feel ready to move onto the next step.

- Lightly touch your fingertips against the opening to the vaginal canal, and breathe here for a few moments, noticing what arises and letting it flow. Notice how your fingers feel to touch your pussy, and how your pussy feels to be touched by your fingers. Stay here until you are ready to move on or if you are feeling complete with this, ending the practice with moving your hands to heart and womb and taking grounding breaths.

- If ready for the next step, apply slightly more pressure with your middle finger to the opening to your Yoni and pause, feeling into what is *arising and arousing you, what is inviting you in VS what is repelling you.*

- Next, begin to explore with this finger and the others, touching your Yoni in various ways, leaning into what kinds of touch invite you to open and soften further. Asking yourself, *"What would feel really good for me to receive through my touch right now? What kind of touch is opening me?"*

- Do this above step for as long as you like, allowing yourself to tune into your intuition and primal instincts, and following what feels good and nourishing to you and your Yoni.

- At any point, if something doesn't feel good, STOP, breathe, and take notice. Remember, there is no rush and no goal to reach. *And you are in control.*

- Now, if you are continuing... come back to a light pressure of fingertips against the opening to the vaginal canal. Ask permission to enter, for example, "Sacred Vessel of my body, divine temple of my birthright, may I enter here?" (use any words that feel good for you) AND WAIT. Wait for as long as it takes until you Hear the answer from within. It may also come as a tension in the body for NO and a relaxation in the body for YES. Also, it is possible to simply KNOW that you are ready to enter. For more clarity on interpreting your body's signals through your senses – see the Awakening Intuitive Gifts, on page 64 of this book).

- If you have received a YES to enter, proceed to the next step. If it is a NO, then stay here until you are ready to move on or if you are feeling complete with this, ending the practice with moving your hands to heart and womb and taking grounding breaths.

- Once you have received the go-ahead signal from your body, which could feel like an opening or release, or an inviting of more Pleasure in, or a curiosity or sense of Play, you are ready to move onto the next step of entering your vaginal canal with your finger or fingers.

- Placing your finger or fingers against the opening to your yoni, gently glide your finger inside, taking as much time as needed, and stopping at any point. You can put part of your finger in or all of it, and anywhere in between. When resistance arises, pause, and breathe, taking as much time as you need.

- Notice your breath and inviting in any sounds, from earlier with the toning practice you did earlier in this practice, or with whatever sounds want to come through you. There is no right or wrong way to do this, as long as you keep following only what is Pleasurable and Joyful.

- If you are complete at this point, end the practice with moving your hands to heart and womb and taking grounding breaths until you feel ready to close the Ceremony.

- If you are continuing, the invitation is to go deeper, reaching the Cervix if it physically is there- it feels like the head of a penis, circular in shape, and the furthest point you can reach at the end of the vaginal canal. You may not be able to reach it fully if you are close to Ovulation (for those that Ovulate) as its position changes. If this is the case, not to worry, remember that there is no goal here, and to remain curious about what is arising and how you are feeling during this process. *The Cervix is the doorway to the Womb Space where the Uterus and hub for creative and life creating activity reside. It is also known as the Gateway to Goddess (read more about the Cervix on page 143).*

- Breathe deeply, letting any sounds, hums, out of your mouth, opening and relaxing your jaw, while exploring the inner femme-scape of your Cervix and vaginal canal with your fingers. Continuing here until you feel complete with the process, and giving yourself permission to STOP at any time, OR to allow your Pleasure to take over and lead you, following the sensations of what feels good in every moment.

- You are complete, at any point that you feel done with the process.

- When you feel ready to close the Ceremony, take a few moments to breathe naturally, just as you began. Allowing any emotions to flow through and being a witness to your beauty and courage.

- If you invited your Ancestral Guides in for support, Thank Them for their guidance.

- To end the Ceremony, you may wish to smoke cleanse the room, blow out the candle, and take some time (now or at a later time) to write down any impressions or reflections.

There are some Reflection Questions below to help you integrate this process.

Reflections

- What has this process shown you about your Sexual Nature and your connection to Pleasure?

- Did you notice any emotions arise during the process? If so, which ones?

- Was there a moment at any point, where you weren't sure of what felt good and what didn't? What insights do you have about why this might be?

- Did touching your body, and specifically, your Pussy (if you did), bring up any shame or guilt for you? Was there something that you did or didn't do that allowed it to move through?

- Do you feel guilt or shame right now about touching yourself? If so, why do you think that is?

- What aspects of this practice were deeply nourishing for you and ones that you'd like to explore more?

If you feel called to share and be witnessed, please reach out to me with any insights or reflections you had about this process, akaiyha@medicinewomenrise.com

An excellent resource for detailed and accurate Women's anatomy, and a guide for continuing to explore your body in possibly new ways, solo and with a partner, is Women's Anatomy Of Arousal, by Sheri Winston.

The Wild Man, Reciprocity, & Sacred Union

In this book, I have focused primarily on Women and the Wild Feminine. However, it is important to note that we cannot achieve Worldwide Freedom from Oppressive Systems, and Reclamation of Sexual Sovereignty, by just addressing one part of humanity; we need, too, to talk about Men, and particularly, about the Wild Masculine.

Just as the Wild Woman and her Reclamation of Sacred Feminine Essence is making an emergence on Earth right now, so, too, is her Divine Masculine counterpart, the *Wild Man*. The Wild Woman knows that the Wild Man's kind of Warrior has been denigrated, shamed, abused, tortured, whipped into submission, and pushed to War by the hyper-masculinized over-culture, severed from his own Feminine Essence, the Goddess who lives in all humans.

We need Wild Men NOW, more than ever, to help bring back the *Honourable Harvest* to our beloved Earth, and for all beings who depend on these Lands for the Circle of Life. We need to re-teach ourselves how to do this, in order to survive, and in order to allow our living planet to thrive, just as our ancient Ancestors did successfully for almost 200,000 years.

Robin Wall Kimmerer writes,

"We need the Honourable Harvest today. But like the leeks and the marten, it is an endangered species that arose in another landscape, another time, from a legacy of traditional knowledge. That ethic of reciprocity was cleared away along with the forests, the beauty of justice traded away for more stuff. We've created a cultural and economic landscape that is hospitable to the growth of neither leeks nor honor. If the earth is nothing more than inanimate matter, if lives are nothing more than commodities, then the way of the Honorable Harvest, too, is dead."

Reciprocity is the Foundation for living in symbiotic relation with all forms of life. It teaches us that "What we reap, we sow" - what we give, we will have returned to us. This is a fundamental ethic, a natural law, that has been forgotten by many, and where we must return, if we are to have Restoration and Reconciliation.

When we take more than we need, when we take without asking permission, and when we take it without respectful Gratitude towards any of our kin - a plant, an animal, a human, or the Earth - we are going against the current of reciprocity, and working against the survival of all.

When our bodies are treated with disrespect and disregard - as anything less than the Sacred vessels that they are - either by ourselves, or by others, we are living outside of reciprocity.

When abuse, a violation of boundaries, occurs against any person, entity, or part of the Earth, Trauma sets into the body. And, unfortunately, whether it is in our own lives or in the lives of others, Trauma begets more Trauma, as the ethic of reciprocity is forgotten and disrespected. The natural world observes and lives by this naturally, and without fail.

Our wild ancestors did not view themselves apart from nature, so it is not surprising that archaeologists have uncovered evidence that our ancient ancestors lived in cyclical, reciprocal relation to the natural world.

How did humanity stray so far from these life-sustaining origins?

Humans, in so-called "civilizations", have been fighting wars for several thousand years, often not knowing what they have been fighting for, told they were fighting for a cause that would help restore balance, when, in reality, they were fighting to fill the pockets of a greedy few, who had long rejected living in reciprocity, who had decided that conquering and owning land, resources, and people (none of which can ever truly be owned) was justified, for the sake of "Power Over".

However, there are signs that indicate that Peace is, in fact, possible, that War and the slave-based systems of oppression that drive disharmony need not, and must not, exist, if we are ever going to find our way back to living in harmonious relations with each other and all beings. We need to adopt the motto: "Just because we can, doesn't mean that we should ", and begin to work together to do better.

It isn't Women alone who are being called upon to navigate the journey back to Reclaiming the Sacredness of Life and Integrating Wholeness; it is Men, as well. If Women were to only do the Healing for themselves, and Men were to not, the issues that we are facing in our families, in our communities, and in places all over the planet, would never be resolved.

It is our *Collective Energy* of Feminine/Masculine, the Sacred Union of these two, living within each of us and between us, that provides the Healing Salve for living harmoniously and in reciprocity. In this respect, our bodies are intended to be just as are all natural bodies, with a balance of these two necessary energies; it is the glorious, synergistic combination that holds the keys to the critical Restoration Process.

We all come to this human experience of life on Earth with both Feminine and Masculine energies as polarities within us. We are born into a body that is a visual and energetic representation of these two primary and fundamental energies, with a Sexual Nervous System that supports the Harmony of one of these as Primary, and one as Secondary.

It is not just in humans where we find the balance of these energies. The dance of Yin (Feminine Essence) and Yang (Masculine Essence) forms the basis for the Natural World, the Cosmos, and the Seasons, as well.

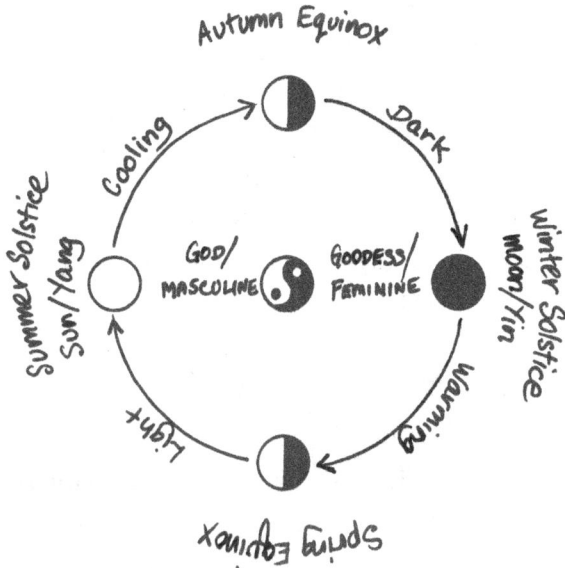

The Wild Man is the Embodied Masculine, the "Warrior". To be clear, when we speak of the "Warrior", this is not in any way referring to the hollowed-out sort of Man who fights Wars for greedy, destruction-based, "Power Over" systems, but rather, the Man who is True to the Sacred Heart of the Warrior. He is the Protector who stands boldly in the face of all oppressive systems, who serves from a place of deep integrity and Wholeness, who shields the innocent from harm, restores Truth and Honour to the Earth, re-establishes the Honourable Harvest, embraces "Power With" rather than "Power Over", and reveres both Goddess and God as equals.

Our Warrior, our Wild Man, is he who lives and loves from his Sacred Heart-and-Cock energy of Penetrative Intelligence and Loving Support. He is the Father who delivers the seed of Life and provides for his family, the Lover who dances with expressive passion, the Brother who links arms with his Wild Woman Sisters and Brothers, refusing to participate in the over-culture's negative views of Women, and a Man of Great Spirit who finds his way to Wholeness and Balance through honouring both the God/Creator and Goddess/Creatrix as equal, and, therefore, his own inner Divine Masculine and Sacred Feminine.

In a world where Trauma continues to pervade everyday life almost all over the Earth, the Wild Man refuses to participate in systems or activities that do not honour reciprocity and the Honourable Harvest. He restores Integrity to structures, where it has been lost or forgotten, and plants seeds where they are welcomed, acknowledging that all of life, including his own, is born from the dance of Sacred Union between Feminine and Masculine, Earth and Sky, Moon and Sun.

The Wild Man may be carrying his own traumas and wounds from childhood – any number of kinds of abuses, violations, crossing of boundaries – that, like the Wild Woman's wounds, affect how he lives and loves, affects his sense of personal Power.

Often within just two days of life outside of his Mother's Womb (sometimes up to 10 days), the young Warrior's body may experience a violation, often done by his parents who may have unwittingly bought into it as both "normal" and "hygienically necessary" - the act of surgical *circumcision*.

The Cock (science refers to it as "the penis"), the testicles, and the Male Sexual Nervous System is a vast network of nerves, much like the Yoni and Womb are for Women - the center of Male Pleasure. The Cock is connected to all organs in the male body through the Nervous System – in fact, it is its central force - and the foreskin has a purpose to act as a protection for the highly sensitive network of nerves running through it. The life-giving lingam is designed to provide the seed of life that grows to a human life within the Woman's Womb.

As the Male sexual energy is usually focused more on his Masculine polarity of giving, than his Feminine polarity of receptivity (but not always), the surgery of circumcision is a Trauma inflicted on *a most Sacred part of his body*. It signals to him not only that the world he has newly entered is a painful and distrustful place to be, but also that his Cock was not perfect as it was created, that some part of his body and its ability to give life was not quite right, needing to be altered.

A man who has had the end of his foreskin cut off, while in a fragile infant state, or at any point later in his young life, may feel emotionally and physically cut off from giving and receiving Pleasure, which is, in fact, his Sacred Birthright. This removal of an integral part of the male body, severs part of the Pleasure connection, desensitizing the penis, and in turn, desensitizes the man himself to parts of his life, especially where his sexuality is concerned. He may become less able to discern what is true for him when it comes to his own Pleasure, let alone being able to interpret the Pleasure needs and responses of his partner. It deeply wounds his Spirit, and diminishes his Power – even if he is not aware of what has happened to him – in the world, and within himself.

The number of circumcisions has been declining in the west since the peak of 90% in the 1950s, but not fast enough; one out of every three infant boys is still being subjected to this invasive surgery.

When we peel away the layers that have allowed and fostered the circumcision of young male children to have emerged and taken hold of social acceptance for the procedure – the more than 100 years of historical entrenchment in the medical community, the (inaccurate) hygienic excuses, the religious moralism that the surgery would keep boys from masturbating, the generational ego pride of "like-father-like-son", and the mean-spirited yet sad "well-if-it-was-good-enough-for-me" kind of posturing – all that is left is the stark, horrendous reality that *circumcision is societally sanctioned genital mutilation*. This systemic assault by the over-culture on our boys' bodies, psyches, and spirits should no longer be acceptable nor permissible. It must stop.

Who could possibly benefit from the removal of Males' Sacred sensory force (in some cases) and the indoctrinated idea that removing a part of a boy's penis is a good idea? We should look no further than those who have sought to control and make soldiers out of our boys and Men to benefit their own greed and "Power Over" all. A Man who is cut-off from his Sacred Cock/Heart connection is easier to convince to fight a war, where, like all wars ever fought, it seeks to destroy and conquer, to control people and other "resources", to rape Mother Earth, and to take what is not given.

With the arrival of the internet in the last few decades, there has been a proliferation of ways that young boys and Men can be bombarded with violent images that glorify killing each other and abusing Women, as well as through pornography- a distortion of the true connection and devotion that can be experienced between Sacred Feminine and Divine Masculine Union.

We are a culture of modern humans lacking in the foundation of Earth Mother and Sky Father Union. We have filled the Lands and the Skies with War Vehicles of destruction and plunder, while living out of touch with reciprocity. If we do not move to heal ourselves and each other, all that will be left will be barren wasteland.

As I have mentioned earlier, in the *Reclaiming Sexual Sovereignty* portion of this book, healing and restoring Wholeness is always possible, even when we have had parts of our bodies - in this case, our Sexual Nervous System - removed without our consent. We are not born with the destiny to live a life half-felt, or one where Trauma needs to give birth to more of its kind. We are born with a destiny of Freedom and Pleasure, and we can Reclaim it any time we decide to. It is the Union of Wild Woman and Wild Man that can help us to move through the Reclamation Process, if we choose to accept the gifts of this Union - first within ourselves, and then, with each other, our partners, and our community.

The Wild Man who wishes to Reclaim his body for his own Pleasure and Power, who is ready to step into his Warrior energy - for the good of himself, his family, his community, the Earth and all of her inhabitants - brings with him the gifts of Sacred Providing and helps to restore the balance of reciprocity.

The Wild Man is he who chooses to make Love with Life, and views Women and the Sacred Feminine as living embodiments of his own inner Feminine nature. When he is welcomed in by the Wild Woman, like her, he submits his Mind, Body, and Spirit to the dance of Sacred Union, the movement of Life Force Energy between the Feminine and Masculine that is anchored in reciprocity. It exists without forcing or coercing, because it is intricately connected to the flow of nature, the seasons, and Life. Reciprocity and Sacred Union teach us to ask Permission, when we want to share any kind of energy with another being, human, plant, or animal kin. When we harvest, that is, when we take or receive something from another being, we need to ask first, and then, wait for the answer. If we do not receive a YES, then we need to accept it as a NO. If we receive shared energy, we need to express our Gratitude respectfully, from the heart.

When the Wild Man makes love to Wild Woman, she feels the potency of his Divine Truth inviting her to soften deeper into her Feminine Essence, Soft Dark Bliss. She melts into a pool of nothingness, liminal space between death and rebirth. Immense waves of deep pleasure come over them both.

If he is given permission to enter her Sacred Passageway, the tip of his Sacred Cock will touch her Cervix, the portal to the Goddess. The sea of endless Pleasure has been entered - bottomless, ever-expanding into unknown spaces, vast like the Cosmos, eternally burning like the Sun, eternally receptive like the Moon.

The Sacred Union of Wild Woman and Wild Man is possible when each of them embodies their own deepest Pleasure and Joy, and then come together in the cosmic Dance of Two. The Wild Joy that is experienced within this union is powerful enough to send ripples out into the Multiverse, sustainable enough to outlast anything that would seek to destroy it, and deeply rooted enough to forever remain in Sacred Feminine and Divine Masculine Love.

All Wars can be traced back to an unnatural, imposed division between these two universal energies, pushing away from reciprocity and accepting a linear, efficient, production- and profit-centered way of thinking and doing.

If we are to reclaim our Wild Joy and experience deep, lasting devotional Love, which is our Sacred Birthright, then we need to put down our weapons - those that we hold in our hands, in our hearts, in our minds, and in our actions - and begin to see each other as the human embodiment of Goddess and God. We need to sit with each other, and let ourselves be seen fully, while we find our way back to living in reciprocity with each other and with Mother Earth.

*A great resource for learning how to give and receive touch that is both pleasurable and consensual is The Wheel of Consent, by Betty Martin. It is a wonderful tool for creating deeper intimacy and learning how to communicate your desires. You can find it on her site at https://bettymartin.org/videos/

*Although this section focused primarily on young boys, it must be noted that there are young girls in our world who are also experiencing socially accepted, indeed, socially expected, horrific genital mutilation through having their clitoris removed, either when they are a baby or at a very young age, to keep them from feeling the Pleasure that is their right to feel.

Eye-Gazing Practice `

- Sit (or lie down) facing your partner
- Close your eyes
- Notice your breath for a few minutes, watching the inhales and exhales come and go without changing anything, letting your body breathe
- When each of you is ready, in your own time, flutter your eyes open and direct your gaze at your partner's left eye – on your right. This is known as the receptive eye or the feminine eye
- There is nothing you need to do, other than focus on their left eye and notice what arises, letting it flow

through; all emotions are ok

- Continue to breathe, and if you notice your breath is feeling restricted, invite some relaxation by focusing on breathing into your lower belly
- Stay here, breathing and gazing at each other's eyes, allowing yourself to be seen and to see your partner beyond words

Dear Brother

I am sorry
for what others have done to you
violated your innocent nature
told you that War is the Way
told you to "be a Man"
"stop crying"
when you were hurting
as a little boy
as an older boy
as a young man
and as a Man

Dear Brother
Wild Soul Brother
You are a Warrior
A Protector of the Innocent
We need you now more than ever

You are a Provider
Holding the Sacred Seeds of Life
In your Divine Body Temple

You are Wholy, Brother
and nothing can change this

The scars and wounds you carry
on your animal body skin
may be those of battle or violation
but, they do not define you
You are Creator
God Embodied
Wild Man
Wise Man
Poet, Lover, Dancer
Sun to the Moon
Son to the Great Mother
King Stag of the Deer
Brother to us All

Naked is Sacred
A Return to Wholeness

One Summer, while continuing to live on wheels and travel on the west coast of British Columbia, we were visiting back home in Ottawa, and I felt a calling to bring Women together in Sacred Spaces of Wild Reclamation and Healing.

I had spent the previous two years learning and integrating what was necessary for my own Healing Journey and Return to Wholeness, steeping myself deeply in Ancient Feminine Wisdom, going into the Underground and facing the depth of my whole being – including the parts of me that I had buried, aspects of myself that I had hidden away, out of fear that others would not accept me. These could no longer remain hidden, if I was going to truly live the life that I had dreamed of.

My eyes and heart had opened to the mystery of the Dark Feminine and her Magick through Womb Wisdom and Ancestral Healing practices, through connecting with my Ancestors and listening to their guidance, and through letting myself be led by the Natural Flow of Life around and within me.

The Sacred Feminine Embodiment practice was some-times hours long, permeating all parts of my day. It wasn't just a practice; it was a way of life. I had learned how to live cyclically, in sync with the Moon's rhythms, and my instincts had amplified greatly.

As I connected and engaged deeply with my inner and outer world in these profound ways, the sensations of every-day life stirred and aroused me, inviting me to step deeper into the Pleasure Palace of my Inner Being that had been awaiting my Homecoming.

It's not that I was new to Pleasure. No. I had been having orgasms since I was a young girl, as young as I can remem-ber, but there was an incident that happened to me - when I was just eight years old - that caused me to reject and push down my ability to take Joy in Pleasure deep inside, to hide it not only from others, but from myself.

I was touched, without my consent or permission, by someone I trusted. I lived with that secret for 20 years of my life, feeling unsafe to say anything about it, and, like most survivors of childhood sexual Trauma, feeling, somehow, like it was my fault. There was so much shame, along with guilt, so I covered it up, and minimized it, feeling powerless to do anything about it.

As an adult, when I finally exposed the abuse, by talking about it, I was told that I was just making it up; I was left on my own - again - without the support of those I loved. This made me regret speaking out, and I didn't bring up the subject again.

The thing about any kind of abuse, though, is that it doesn't go away; try as we do to keep it hidden, it finds a way to come out, and it's often not in a way that we would like.

This one incident (that I could remember) of abuse that happened to me when I was a little girl created Trauma that got trapped in my body, in my Heart, Womb, and Yoni. It affected my Throat and my ability to speak, particularly to be able to share what had happened, and that led to me feeling closed off from the world.

This abuse laid the foundation for my experience with Boys, Men, and the Masculine in me, as well as my ability to connect with Girls, Women, and my Inner Feminine.

The abuse was a major contributing factor to how I felt about myself as a female. At a young age, this act by someone who was in a position of trust, responsibility, "power over"/authority, and who abused my faith in love, had told me that I was only good for someone else's pleasure, that my happiness didn't matter as much as protecting those who chose to harm me and to knowingly violate my innocence.

The incident also affected future sexual encounters, my decision to get married young to someone whom I barely knew, and how I experienced the births of my children.

Leaving my first marriage, at the age of 28, felt like the

hardest thing I had ever done up to that point. It was the beginning of my awakening to my Inner Wild Woman and letting her lead me back to Wholeness.

Later, losing the business, selling everything that we
owned, traveling away from my older children who were at
home with their father, and living in a trailer for two years, felt
like another Initiation by the Wild Woman. I was going
against everything I had been brought up to believe - that
good Mothers and good Women don't do those things, that
we should stay unhappily married for our kids, or stay in one
place and settle down. I had been carrying shame, guilt, and
grief around in my body since I was a child, and they were
covering up what I needed to bright to light, to experience
true, lasting Freedom.

It was creating that space for myself, and venturing somewhere unfamiliar, that provided the container for going into
the depths of my being, listening to my inner knowing, following it, and healing, while not needing to please anyone,
or do anything that I didn't want to do. This doesn't mean that
all Women need to leave their partners or families to know
the Wild Woman, but, for me, even as difficult as it was, it was
the exact thing that I needed. The more I went into the spaces within, where I had locked away those shadows of my
past that I had had a hard time facing, the more deeply
rooted I became - into the Earth, into my Life, and back into
my Pleasure.

I began to realize that I wasn't just doing this for myself; I
was doing this for the benefit of other Women, too. From my

years being a Personal Trainer, Posture Specialist, Energy Healer, Meditation Teacher, and Space Holder, I knew there were other Women who had had similar Trauma experiences as me, because Women often shared their stories. I was seeing now that, regardless of how much effort was put into healing the "issues in the tissues", and especially in the Womb and Pussy, it wasn't effective in our overall health, if we didn't address the Root of the issue - if we didn't go back to the beginning of the Trauma and integrate what had happened. We can't meditate or "high vibe" our way through Sexual Trauma. We need to go back to the source of the issue, where it resides in our body, and Reclaim the Sacred Space as our own.

The practices I had learned through my Womb Wisdom Studies, and many that I had naturally and intuitively felt guided to do through my body's Wisdom, provided the true Healing that I needed to Reclaim my Sexual Sovereignty for myself, and to be able to share it with whomever else I chose. A combination of Cyclical Wisdom, Womb Steaming, Breast/Womb/Yoni Massage, Yoni Egg Practices, Self-Inquiry and Journaling, Ceremony and Ritual, Plant Medicine, Medicine Song, Forest and Ocean Bathing, Ancestral Prayer and Connection, Breathwork, Emotional Release, and Ecstatic Dance, Sacred Sexuality Partner Practices, learning how to speak and honour my Boundaries, how to share my Desires, and the loving devotion of my Man to join me on this journey – these were the Medicine that I needed to bring me back Home to my Wild Sacred Self, and Reclaim the Joy and Pleasure that had been my Birthright all along.

I was beyond ready and excited to share these practices with other Women whom I knew would benefit. I knew that a Sacred Circle would be a safe space to share and reached out to Women in my community. So, on a summer evening of reverence and sisterhood, 13 of us came together in Circle, in our raw and naked vulnerability. We set offerings on the Altar, breathed, released, steamed our Wombs, Yoni-worshiped, sang Medicine Songs, and danced naked around the fire under the stars. Every woman appeared to me as an absolute GODDESS; I was in awe of how much beauty and power there was in these Women. "Our clothes are really lying to us," I thought to myself.

Any remnants of the patriarchal, colonial, hierarchical stories and the accompanying Sister Wounds quickly evaporated, and Healing and Wholeness replaced them. I felt the potency of the Medicine we were sitting with, and I knew, deep within me, that I had answered a call that my Ancestors before me had answered. I had received an important Initiation, reclaiming my Inner Earth Priestess, and I knew that I needed to continue bringing Women together like this, and to create waves out into the Collective for Healing and Remembrance.

Back on the west coast, as our family traveled over the next year-and-a-half, I met many Women who became Sisters almost instantly, and felt a resonance with these offerings. They invited me to share these practices with their communities, and this created many opportunities to sit with Women in Circle, each one solidifying the deeper truths than the one before. I began to hear the same story over and over, with slightly different details – Trauma to the Womb and Pussy. On one occasion, during a Wild Women Retreat, a group of 22 of us gathered in Circle. The space felt deeply contained and safe for sharing. After we had gone through a workshop on Cyclical Living, we took turns sharing what was coming up to be witnessed by our Sisters. Woman after woman shared intimate details about Sexual Trauma, Abuse, and Sister and Mother Wounds, some letting us know that they had never told this to anyone else, that they had kept it hidden, out of fear, shame, or confusion.

It was undeniable, any doubt that I was alone in my experience or that other Women could not relate to what I had been through, vanished. I felt a deep sadness in me, that so many Women had carried this around in their bodies, afraid to speak it, unsure of how to release it, for so long. What awoke in me was a deeper passion than ever before to continue offering the Retreats, Circles, and ways for Women to come together and share their stories, as well as provide a space that we could celebrate our Wholeness and connect deeply to Pleasure as a source of Renewal and Vitality.

When we feel safe with other Women, the depths we are able to reach together, can be greater than what we can experience individually, and taps into a well of Ancient Knowledge - stories vast and diverse, yet many telling a story of the body.

Regardless of what our Body and Spirit have endured, we have the capacity to Heal. Our own touch is healing for our bodies - the fingers, lips, and genitalia bursting with the highest amounts of nerve receptors in the entire landscape of our skin's wonderland. Our Voices are Healing too, speaking our truth, sharing what we have kept hidden for so long, setting ourselves Free from shame and guilt. When we gather with other Women, and we Love ourselves in ways that perhaps we haven't experienced before, we all benefit from being both the witness and the witnessed in that Transformation. Each Circle brings a gift, each Sister is a Teacher, and I honour those who join in, knowing the Courage and Vulnerability that it takes.

During those years of Reclamation, sitting in Circles with many Women, with each one sharing a story of her body, my own body was speaking to me in ways that felt new, yet somehow familiar. Embracing a Cyclical Life, living with the Seasons and Nature as my Guide, had attuned my senses to knowing what I needed in my Life, and what I no longer needed. Sitting with Women who had bodies of different shapes, sizes, ages, and colours, with stories and gifts to share, gave me the exact Medicine that I needed to make a big decision about my own body's well-being. I would have the breast implants that I had been carrying around for too long removed. It had been 13 years since I had felt the heart of my Man beating against my own heart - a silicone wall between us. My youngest son had never laid on my chest without those lumps there, and, for my older children, it had been most of their lives.

In November, on a downward descent into the Earth, as the last of the leaves were falling from the trees, in the Season of letting go, the implants would be leaving my body. I knew that Nature would orchestrate this process for me, if I let myself surrender to it. My Ancestors guided me through the process, and I felt them closer than I ever had. I could feel how proud and happy they were for me, and one Grand Mother Ancestor held my hand while I had the implants removed.

I chose to have the surgery using only local anesthetic, because I wanted to be fully present, a witness to this important part of my journey. During the procedure, the surgeon removed both implants, one that was intact, and one that had been ruptured in my body for an unknown amount of time. The trauma of finding a leaky implant inside my body, while awake on the operating table, and the Healing and Integration Process of accepting my natural breasts, and processing what they had been through, required time and the right environment.

I spent the next few months guided by Wise Woman Energy and allowing myself to rest and heal, supported by the outer Winter environment of slowing down, while nestled in a small house on 75 Acres of Forest at the darkest time of the year, providing endless support and regenerative medicine for the journey forward. I returned to the beautiful and healing self care practice of breast massage weeks after surgery, as it had been so instrumental in showing me what I needed to see and feel, leading me back home to the Wholeness that was there all along, and my sacred naked self.

Dancing Wolves

Women dance with their hands
their hips
energetic kiss

They twirl and twist
bend and snake
hiss and howl
quake and shake

I call them my sisters and they call me the same
there's a love in the air that cannot be explained

It goes beyond societal conditioning or beliefs
Like the depths of the ocean or the moon's dark sleep
Spinning seasons
Turning wheels
When sisters gather and dance we all heal

Breast Massage Practice

Allow this practice to be as intuitive as possible. I give some guidance and structure here to get you started, but it is you that knows best what you need. Listen to your hands, your breath, the sounds of your body for what she likes and doesn't like in terms of being touched. There is no limit to what you can do with this practice. Make it your own and stay curious. There is so much treasure in the Pleasure of your touch.

- Set your space with candles and incense, or anything that will bring a sense of Ceremony into the space.
- Ensure that you are warm and comfortable.
- Place warm hands on your breast area. You may wish to use oil, infused with flowers and herbs or any carrier oil. I prefer castor oil mixed with some almond or jojoba - adding some essential oils that feel opening and inviting if you are feeling called.
- Take some time to settle into your breath and body fully, take as long as you need.
- Begin with sending the energy of love from your heart through your arms and hands into your breasts.
- Breathe deeply into this space, offering prayers of love and gratitude for this area of your body.
- Allow an intention for this practice to arise from within your heart space. *What do you wish to let go of or call into your life? Take your time to hear the response arise.*
- When ready, begin with massaging away from the center to the outside areas of the breast, in a circular motion - this is representing the energy of letting go. You may find

it helpful to tune into what you would like to let go of when doing the motion away from the heart.

- Continue as long as feels right, taking pauses when needed and especially when you feel energy rise to the surface to be released. Give it space to leave.
- Once it feels complete, take a pause and breathe, noticing how you feel.
- When ready, reverse the direction of energy flow, moving your hands from the outer edges of your breast area, toward the center in circular movements, gathering your breast tissue in your hands toward the heart. This is the energy of calling in and receiving.
- Follow the pace and touch that feels good, taking your time and pausing where you need to.
- Take your time, remembering to breathe, noticing any emotions that are arising, Grief, Sadness, Joy, Pleasure etc, allowing them space to move through and be witnessed.
- You can choose now to focus on one side or area at a time, using your intuition to guide you, or you can end the practice here, placing your hands on your breast area and saying loving words to your body: "Thank You, I Love You, You are Beautiful", telling your body all of the things you love about her and feeling her Gratitude for this time you put aside for this practice.
- If you are continuing with one side, begin at the underarm area at the side of your ribs, and move your hand/s in strokes toward the heart area, gathering the breast tissue toward the center. You may wish to add in other movements that feel releasing and nourishing, following what feels good for your breast area.

- When that first side feels complete, move to the other side and begin the same process here, taking your time, following your body's feedback and cues. Remember that it should not be painful or feel rushed. Notice your breath and make sure to take your time, going slow.
- When this feels complete, you are ready to close the Ceremony, placing your hands on your breast area and saying loving words to your body: "Thank You, I Love You, You are Beautiful", telling your body all of the things you love about her and feeling her Gratitude for this time you put aside for this practice.
- You may wish to do some reflection writing in your journal through *Automatic Writing Practice* (page 40 of this book) or writing down some insights that came through during this practice. There are some Reflections below to help guide this process.

Reflections

- How did it feel to touch your breasts or breast area (if one or both breasts have been removed) in this intentional way? Did it bring up anything for you about your connection to your breasts/breast area or your heart?

- Did you notice any moments of hesitation or tension arise? If so, where and at what point? Did this bring an awareness that you needed to witness?

- How do you feel about your breasts/breast area, their appearance, feel, look?

- What ideas or beliefs do you have about what your breasts and those of other Women are intended for? Has this practice shifted any of those ideas or beliefs?

- Is this a practice you could see yourself doing regularly? If so, how often? If not, why?

- How were you feeling in your overall energy and mood previous to beginning this practice? How are you feeling after this self-massage practice?

The following questions are for Women who have had breasts or breast tissue removed in surgery:

- Did having one or both of your breasts (or part of) removed, have an impact on your connection to your breast area? If so, how? Are you aware of anything that you are holding onto (anger, resentment, or other) that has kept you from loving your breasts/breast area as it is now? And are you ready to let that go?

- Did this self-massage practice give you a sense of Wholeness about your breast area and body? If not, why do you feel that might be?

- This is an invitation to write a letter in your journal to your body and breasts or breast area (present or past tense), sharing how you feel about this area of your body, creating a space to let go, release, expressing any anger, rage, or other emotions that may want to come through to be witnessed. You can also do the *Intuitive Writing Practice* (page 40 of this book) to allow space for whatever needs to be said, without judgment.

- Placing a hand or two on your heart space, Is there a message that your body needs to share with you now, about the surgery or any part of your breast's journey through life? If so, what is the message?

When you are feeling complete with the Reflection process, you may wish to hold a Fire Ceremony to honour the Sacred pathway you have taken and to release what no longer is needed for your journey ahead.

Fire Release Ceremony

The *Fire Release Ceremony* can be done following the Breast Care Practices, or as a stand-alone Ceremony for anything you wish to let go of, surrender to, or accept and Love, as Fire is an alchemical force that has the power to Heal and Transform. By placing a paper in the fire with words that we have written, and acknowledging what is no longer needed for the next steps of our journey, we imbue the process of transformation with what is Sacred for us. If there are certain releases that came through with the *Automatic Writing Process* in the *Breast Care Practice* or in any of the other Reflection areas of this book, the element of Fire can be called upon to bring a sense of completion, endings, and create a new pathway forward through the alchemical process.

For this process, you will need a place to build a fire out-side (taking into consideration safety precautions), or an in-door or outdoor wood burning fireplace, some paper for writing, or paper that you've already used to write some-thing on that you wish to release in this Ceremony.

You can do this process alone, or with others, as it can be very powerful to be witnessed tossing the paper into the fire, and if you feel called, saying the words written *out loud* before placing the paper in the fire.

Once you have made your fire, you are ready to enter into this Ceremony with yourself or others.

- Take a moment to set your intentions, either individually or with a group. You may wish to state the intentions out loud and be witnessed, or keep them to yourself. Give yourself permission to honour what feels right for you.
- You may wish to call in your Ancestors, asking that they Guide you through the process, and that they offer their Love and Protection to all who are participating. There is an *Ancestral Healing Prayer* located on page 235 of this book for you to include if you feel called.
- If you are coming to this Ceremony without having writ-ten anything, that is fine, and you can take this opportu-nity to write down what you would like to let go, release, heal, or transform at this time. Take as much time as you need to let the words flow. Remember, to be clear on what it is that is no longer serving you and to write it down. This could be ideas or beliefs around body image, aging, being a Woman, Motherhood, Sexuality, or any

area of your life where you may be feeling stuck and wanting to create a powerful shift in the direction of the life you desire. Write all of it down and let the words flow onto the paper.

- Take some time to feel into what you have written on the paper, allowing the energy of your words to come to life, knowing that you are about to alchemize them with the power of fire.

- When ready, take a step toward the fire, stopping before you get there, and reading one last time (out loud or to yourself) what you have written down.

- Take a deep breath and feel the sense of release that will come with letting this go, the sense of Freedom that the fire is able to provide.

- Now, when you are ready, place the paper in the fire, watching it transform and catch into flames. Feel this inner transformation occurring at the same time, freeing you and your energy up, creating more space for inviting in all of the beautiful experiences you deeply desire.

- Take a moment to appreciate yourself for what you have had the courage to do, to write, to share, to voice, and to release. *You are an amazing alchemist, a Priestess of Fire that transforms her pain into Pleasure, and isn't afraid to let her Power be known!*

- You may wish to say words to acknowledge that this process is complete for you, something such as, "And, So It Is!". Perhaps if you are with others, they could also repeat this after you say it, "And, So It Is!", or anything else that feels aligned with this process for you and the group (if present).

- If you are with others, take turns doing this process, one

at a time, each one following the above steps or whatever feels right.

- When you, and others (if present) have completed the
  process, close the Ceremony with a prayer or offering of
  Gratitude for the element of fire, giving Thanks to your
  Ancestors and the Land that you are on for holding you
  and supporting you.

Sister, you're not broken

Sister, you're not broken
You never were and you never will be

Your bones are Earth
Your breath the Wind
You dance in Fire
And shed the Skin

Your body is a perfect Goddess Form
With rolling hills and quaking storms

With Oceans deep and Valleys wide
You are the embodiment of all things Wild
Throw away the ups…
The push-ups
The sit-ups
The put-ups
The one-ups

They're not your Sacred Space
Let your body lead you to your own Pleasure Place

The Temple of Worship begins within
Your moans and prrrs a Sacred Hymn

Sing to the Great Mother who knows your Heart
She's been here all along, from the start

Holding you through all of the seasons
Through the wholeness of your expression,
your Sacred Weaving

Sister you're not broken
You've been opened to life,
It's an expansion of your Being
Because the old way didn't fit right

The Wise Woman / Crone
The Nutritive Soil

"What I do here matters. Everybody lives downstream. My pond drains to the brook, to the creek, to a great and needful lake. The water net connects us all. I have shed tears into that flow when I thought that motherhood would end. But the pond has shown me that being a good mother doesn't end with creating a home where just my children can flourish. A good mother grows into a richly eutrophic old woman, knowing that her work doesn't end until she creates a home where all of life's beings can flourish."
~Braiding Sweetgrass, Robin Wall Kimmerer

Death as Medicine

Without death, there cannot be new life and growth. Life is not linear, but cyclical, the seasons being the foundation of our experience here. Just as the Earth goes through her cycles, so does the Cosmos - as above, so below. We live in a world of polarity and opposites, ever changing, ever evolving. Death is a doorway to the next phase, and a space to rest before beginning again. When we rush the natural process of death, bypassing winter, we rob ourselves of this necessary transformation that comes from letting go and sending the nutrients that we have gathered throughout our lifetime into the Earth. All of nature knows death and hon-ours it as intrinsic to the fabric of life.

Since the beginning, and throughout ancient times and cultures, we Women have lived by the cycles of The Moon. We would gather and bleed together at the New Moon, and as oracles received important insights and visions, this would help support the tribes and communities that we were part of. Women, as receptors in our energy, would lis-ten, be still, and receive the wisdom of life through our Wombs, hearts, and spirits. Our elder Women, our Crones, who had entered the "beyond-bleeding years", held a spe-cial place in these communities, and were revered as Medicine Women, who, having spent much of their earlier years birthing, bleeding, and gathering their medicine bun-dles of experiences and wisdom, were teachers and guides to the younger Women. Our ancient Crones were the Wise Women, carrying the sacred knowledge from the past, and ensuring that it was seeded into the future, that celebrations of the Menarche, and other important rites of passage for young Women, were integral with the natural laws that govern all of life. These ancient ones had witnessed and embodied more of life experiences than the younger Women, and were looked upon with as much reverence as the oldest trees in the forest: Wise, Magickal, Wondrous.

We Women have always had an internal compass for nurturing in our systems, in our bodies. This energy also ensures the safety and sovereignty of our babies, both literal and figurative. As we step into the Crone years, this need to nurture the future grows, spreading out to include care for grandchildren, or for the world at large, as well as for our creative projects and those we mentor. We are never done mothering, if we don't want to be, sending ripples out into our communities and the world.

As we move through the macro cycles of life - Maiden, Mother, Wild Woman, and finally Wise Woman/ Crone - we progressively focus less and less of our attention on the opinions of others, drawing deeper from the well of inner confidence and strength. This is a time where we can come into our true power, and access our voice like never before, both during our micro cycle of our bleeding time, and during stages of loss, death, and grieving during the macro cycle of our lives.

The Crone embodies the wisdom from the previous cycles, both micro and macro, and retains her blood, for ultimate wisdom and healing power.

The Celtic Goddess, The Cailleach, is a caretaker of the underworld and nurturer of roots, and who brings winter upon The Land, and watches over the last phase of the cycle. She is the intermediate - the Governess of the in-between realms, the Priestess of liminal spaces between death and rebirth, the Dark Moon Goddess who governs the Dark Moon phase when the Moon disappears for 3 days per cycle. She oversees us during the bleeding time of our menstrual cycle, the end of a cycle that is preparation for the next one which will rebirth us energetically and physically.

In our macro cycle of life, she comes to us when we no longer are bleeding, when we feel ready to embrace all of the wisdom from the previous life cycles of Maiden, Mother, and Wild Woman. She doesn't necessarily become the main force that we embody right after we are beyond bleeding, but she is there waiting when we are ready to welcome her fully and accept her gifts.

The Crone has been bled out by society. She has been used up and tossed aside by over-culture or told that she needs to be more - more plump, more Maiden like, more Mother like, more, more, more.

In the last several thousand years, as patriarchy rose, it was the Crone who was seen as an enemy who stood in the way of an overtaking and colonization. She became the enemy to those who would take what was not theirs to take, without permission or Gratitude, without consciousness rooted in Love. We Women were told that we were only good for birthing and for catering to our husband and family.

Over thousands of years, the view of our older Women changed dramatically, reducing these holders of Wisdom to being seen as useless if they couldn't reproduce, or, at least, produce. This was much like how humanity's views shifted about The Land, from belonging to the collective and the commons, from abundance, and from following the cycles of nature, to the acceptance of the concepts of ownership of The Land, to the prevailing viewpoint of lack and scarcity, and to a production that was imposed upon The Land. Along with agriculture's new concept of male land owner-ship came an expanded idea of hierarchy and ownership - of Women, of children, of other men, and of material "re-sources" and goods - chattel! This fundamental, distorted Masculine shift to the view of Women, property, competi-tion, and hierarchy would eventually lead to the establish-ment of the patriarchal Abrahamic religions, that would eventually put our Wild Women into cages, and kill our Wise Women.

The Crone knows that The Land, people, and so-called "resources" can never truly be owned, that these are gifts, and that we cannot truly own anything that we are not able to take with us through the death door. As the gatekeeper, the Crone's wisdom is a reminder of this truth.

The Crone in ancient times was revered and highly re-spected as a deep wisdom keeper and she was a respected elder in her tribe or community. Just as the oldest tree in the forest holds a great power and energy that the others look to for guidance and support, so too does the Crone hold this same big Mother Love.

The Wise Woman's depth cannot be measured by our current systems of measurement. She is like the depths of the ocean that have been unexplored, making homes for the unwanted and desolate creatures who come to her for refuge. She hides in the subterrain of our hearts, wombs, and minds, knowing she has been forgotten by many, yet resting in a faith as deep as the deepest roots that everything is a cycle, and she is never truly forgotten. Her wisdom is profound and simple; she doesn't need to prove herself to anyone. Her softness is unparalleled, her courage unwavering, she is the GrandMother, The Great Mother, The Mother of all Mothers. She has birthed, breathed, and bled, died over and over again, and each time she has come back to life, timeless, all-renewing.

Reflections

- What ideas have you held in the past, or that you have been holding more recently about aging and older Women?

- What, if anything, concerns you about the way that older people, especially Women, are treated in society right now, and, potentially, may still be in play when you are in your Crone/ Wise Woman phase?

- Answer one of the two following questions:

A. If you are not yet in your Crone years, what are you look-
    ing forward to, as the advantages about being a Crone,
    and why? What are you afraid of about being a Crone,
    and why?

OR

B. If you are already in your Crone years, what do you know
    to be the advantages and benefits about being a Crone
    so far? What are you looking forward to, and why? What
    are you afraid of about being at this phase in life, and
    why? Do you feel that you have settled deeply into the
    Power of your Wisdom? If not, what is holding you back
    from stepping into it?

*   What are the beliefs and attitudes that underlie the
    above set of questions, and where do you think they
    come from?

*   What sorts of things do you notice about a Crone / Wise
    Woman who has embraced this phase of her life and her
    Power? How could you /can you own the Wise Woman
    phase of your own life?

Healing "The Witch Wound"

As the Christian Church invaded Europe with the Roman soldiers, the statues, temples and symbols of the Mother Goddess were destroyed, burned, and buried, and strong attempts were made to do the same to her stories. The idea of "original sin" that was supposed to have been perpetrated by Eve, was spread throughout the conquered lands by the Christian Church to control Women, to make us small and obedient, and to shut us up.

However, after centuries, these old ways remained in the hearts and daily lives of the conquered people. The patriarchal leaders of the power-hungry Christian Church became frustrated in their efforts to dominate and control the population, to be able to create the submissiveness and controllability that they wanted.

And then they decided that they knew what the problem was: Women, especially strong Women, the Wise Women or "peasant healers". The experience and knowledge of herbal remedies to treat the sick that had been passed down from generation to generation, and of midwifery practices learned through the millennia of assisting with birthing, were a threat to the religious messages they preached. The more successful these Women were, the more the Church noticed that people were less reliant on prayer to the Christian God. It was deemed that their competition, the Wise Women, had to go.

In 1484, citing an excerpt from Bible (Exodus 22:18) that

states, "Thou shalt not suffer a witch to live", Pope Innocent VIII gave Church officials, in all locations throughout its dominion - wherever there was resistance to the Church from the culture - the authority to hunt out "witches" and, by whichever manner they saw fit, kill them, without any hearing or trial. A hate-filled, misogynistic book, whose title translates from German as *Hammer of the Witches,* stoked these fires that were meant to demonize Women, especially powerful Women, and their powers.

Women of any age who held nature-based, Mother Goddess beliefs that differed from the Christian view of Women, Women who stood in their power and wisdom – and particularly the Women of Crone years – were targeted for annihilation. The goal was to break the ties of ancestry, spirituality, customs, traditions, ceremony, celebration, and community, so that the people would buckle to the power of the Church.

To make their point forcefully, "Ordinary" punishments would not do, in this case, as witchery was named as an "exceptional crime" apart from any other crime. Accused Women were taken from their homes, imprisoned, stripped, tortured, hanged, burned, and drowned. In the records that were both created and held by the "victors" - the men and the systems who held power - we are told today that they indicate that 40,000 Women of power were killed during the Witch Hunts - a reign of terror that went on for 200 years - while hundreds of thousands were arrested. Different estimates set the number from 8,000,000 to 9,000,000. Regardless of the number that represents the truth, this was femicide or "gendercide" - as named by Erica Jong - on an organized scale that the world had never seen before, nor has witnessed since. It is no coincidence that the Church then began to support the training of males in medicine, who could only be given license to practice medicine *by the Church itself.*

There were many reasons a Woman could be accused of being a witch: gathering with others without the presence of a church official; making medicine; communing with plant and animal spirits, including talking to an animal; owning a cat; having knowledge of how to birth or to prevent conception; any form of sexual play or sensual display, including experiencing pleasure and orgasm – even with their husbands; and any other obscure reason the accusers could concoct.

Women who had chosen not to marry, especially those in their Wise Woman stage of life (their Crone beyond-bleeding and birthing years), were especially targeted for accusations of witchcraft, for they embodied most, if not all, of the "crimes" listed above, while in their position of leadership to the Women of their communities. By killing these Wise Women, the ancient beliefs and knowledge - of the Earth, of nature-based healing, and of the connection to the Divine Feminine - would go with them.

.The Witch Hunts also became a tool to sweep away those widowed Women who had decided not to remarry and who occupied valuable land that, by law, they were not allowed to own. By accusing them of witchery, what had been their husband's land could be taken.

The merciless persecutors of this powerful patriarchal institution found ways – both by overtly violent and insidious means – to get Women to turn against other Women, to name others in their community as witches. Out of fear of being persecuted themselves, many did just that. Poisonous fear gripped the communities, and Women retreated from each other, from their communities, and even from themselves and from their own powers.

This created a massive wound, a further rupture in the collective heart of the people of Earth, and it still exists in our world today as a disconnection from the Sacred Feminine essence in all of us Women. It has created the "Witch Wound" or "Sister Wound" that can be an obstacle between Women.

When we are blocked from the energy of our Sacred Feminine essence, it cannot flow through the body, just as a river would flow to the ocean, back to the Source to then cycle back through again. This means that the energy that we have available to us, to create the life we want, cannot be fully realized and birthed into reality, since this blockade or dam is standing in the way.

If we feel that we didn't receive the support that we needed growing up to become the Woman that we were destined to be, if we feel that our female peers, friends, sisters, or Women at large were not supportive of our own unfolding and of our creations, especially in crucial initiatory periods like that of our First Moon cycle, we can still be carrying the wound or feeling of something being incomplete.

This feeling of incompleteness is also a feeling of lack or "not-enough-ness", and it can leave a wound in the Sacred centers of mind, heart, womb, and pussy. We may seek to salve this wound in any number of ways:

- Seeking attention in negative ways (such as through mis-aligned sexual encounters that do not honour our boundaries or deepest held desires)
- Gossiping
- Comparing ourselves to other Women
- Comparing other Women to each other
- Buying things that we don't need or even truly want
- Using substances, or enabling other kinds of addictions
- Tuning out of our relations
- Treating our bodies with disregard by pushing ourselves too hard or not giving ourselves enough of what we need to be healthy
- Engaging in any behaviour that does not truly foster deep, nutritive relations to our bodies and to each other.

We are in times of massive energetic shifts and healing, and these wounds are being called up to be healed in each of us, as well as in the collective.

When we Women share our stories in Circle, it is often the first step we go through to feel that we are accepted for who we truly are, enabling us to heal the wounds that have been keeping us from experiencing a deeper, intimate con-nection with each other.

Women's Circles remind us of our Wholeness, our perfection as we are, allowing for true, deep healing. When there is nothing to fix, only Love remains. When we are ready to let down our guard, and move past what has happened before this moment, and open our arms to life as it was meant to be, we see each other clearly and we know that we are each a radiant Goddess Embodied.

An excellent resource for learning about Women's suppressed "her-stories" and "Restoring Women to Cultural Memory" is through the Suppressed Histories Archives created by Max Dashu at https://www.suppressedhistories.net ."She has built a collection of some 50,000 images and 100 visual presentations, as well as producing numerous articles, photo essays, books, and videos fleshing out the cultural heritages that have been hidden from us."

Reflections

- Do you feel anything arise when you think about feminine wounding in your life, either those that you have received or that you have inflicted?

- How have wounds of the feminine kept you from showing up in your authentic expression?

- When have you felt *most* supported by and connected to other Women? Why?

- Is there a desire that you notice is yearning for a deeper connection with Women? If so, what support systems are in place already, groups, circles, in your community that offer a space to connect with Women? Is this something you feel like exploring further? Or even creating yourself?

If you are looking for help and guidance with creating a Women's Circle in your Community, reach out to me at akaiy-ha@medicinewomenrise.com for more info on how we can help you!

Wisdom of Blood

As our hormones drastically shift during the luteal phase of the Inner Wild Woman, just before we bleed, she holds the keys for us to be able to enter the Underground next, where we will go into the darker parts of our own psyche, along with the collective psyche of Women and of humanity, where we may have buried the bones of the past long ago.

Then, with Wild Woman gone, we go downward into the Earth, into the dark chambers of our deepest held remembering, where the Crone or Wise Woman is waiting for us to visit her in tunneled-out caves of the Earth, to mingle with the unseen, and to make peace with the parts of ourselves that we have shut away, buried deep down, hoping that we would never have to deal with them again. Because life is cyclical, we can never truly be free of something that we shove down in the depths; it will unconsciously rule our lives, until we go down there and sit with it, facing what we couldn't before.

The Dark Feminine Goddesses - Wild Woman, Priestess, Medicine Woman, Crone, Witch, Wise Woman, and Enchantress (among many others) - symbolize the darker aspects of Women's lives in a wholly embodied way. Many of us Women have been taught to fear these aspects of ourselves, to hide them away, and, instead, to "turn to the light for salvation and truth". However, this can lead to an even bigger wound, and, inevitably, we encounter the Dark Goddess during a *dark night of the soul*.

All of this is imprinted and stored in our blood. Leading up to our bleeding time, during the inner seasons of spring, summer, and fall, our blood carries the remnants of the entire cycle, helping us to transition into winter, and truly let go of that which is dying - outdated programming, beliefs, stressful lifestyles, and habits that aren't healthy. When we have a difficult time letting go, it doesn't all leave with our monthly blood, so some can remain in the body, known as "old blood". This blood can show up in the next cycles as spotting, dark brown, leading up to our bleeding time, and is the body's way of clearing out that which we have carried the longest first. Being out of sync with our natural way of being - that is, the way that we feel best in our bodies and spirits - can lead to larger issues, if left unattended. Of course, this old blood, or spotting, does not always reveal the source of the issue and some deeper exploration and reflection may be necessary.

Our blood is wise, holding the memories of our own past, of our lineage, our ancestors, as well as showing us our internal rhythms, keeping time with those of nature, and pointing us to what could be out of alignment, what may need tending.

It holds memories of old ways that we may have forgotten, ways that we wish to hold onto or rekindle in ourselves, passing down to our children and keeping alive in our families. Our blood is healing, fortifying, nourishing; there is so much healing power in our blood.

If we are still in our bleeding years, we can tune into our blood and its messages, and get curious ….

- What colour is it?
- Does it appear to be healthy?
- It is flowing and rich in red colour?
- Is it stagnant, sparse, or heavy?
- How does it smell? Taste?
- Does it bring relief in our emotions, heart, mind, and womb when we bleed?
- Does bleeding feel grounding? Depleting? Overwhelming?
- How can we honour this blood that comes with the tides of The Moon, and the gift it brings?
- What are the gifts?
- What is our relation to our blood?
- Do we see it as a nuisance or a blessing?

Just as The Moon has influence over the tides of the ocean, she also has influence over our bodies, because Women are water beings. Our ancient tribes knew the powerful connection between Women and The Moon, worshiping female deities and Goddesses, like Hekate, one of the most ancient, predating all male deities and masculine-dominant religions. The ancient ones knew the sacredness of blood, were never squeamish or disgusted by it. Blood is the nectar of life, running through the rivers of our veins, bringing nourishing oxygen and nutrients to all of our cells. Our blood restores us to wholeness.

Our blood can be an offering to the Earth, given during our bleeding time, at the base of a tree, into a stream, a lake, river, the ocean, wherever there is a space that feels sacred to us.

Our blood can be offered ceremonially as an offering to let go and heal. We can intentionally channel our heart's desire and give our blood back to the Earth in gratitude. It can be an offering from our heart and our womb into our Mother, a gift of gratitude. As we release our blood into the Earth, we can say prayers and words of thanks, drumming, singing, and chanting.

Blood is a blessing. We are wiser and clearer during this time - unafraid to make choices that we know need making, ready to cut ties and strings with what we feel is already dying.

Akaiy'ha

We accept death as necessary for rebirth,
rest is necessary for vitality,
letting go is necessary for growth.

The Crone and our blood teach us that life is precious and not to be wasted, that we can intentionally reflect on death as a way to infuse our days with greater Joy and Love.

How many winters do we have here? Nobody knows.
How many cycles do we get? Impossible to tell.

Knowing that our existence is only temporary, and the time we have is unknown, we value each moment, we let go of petty grievances that are keeping us held in old patterns; we embrace death as the inevitable, and we bloom to our fullest potential, knowing that this, too, will end. Like the Phoenix, an ancient symbol of rebirth, we, too, are reborn anew each cycle; new beginnings formed from the ashes, we rise and move forward once again.

"Here you will give your gifts and meet your responsibilities. To become naturalized is to live as if your children's future matters, to take care of the land as if our lives and the lives of all our relatives depend on it. Because they do."

~ Braiding Sweetgrass, Robin Wall Kimmerer

Weaving Wholeness

Each person and their family members reflect their inheritance of learned behaviours, traumas, conditioning, genetic traits, characteristics, personalities, and family themes, opening a doorway into their ancestry, potentially mending the pain of the past. Whether through nature or nurture, the patterns are woven into the fabric of family stories, back to the beginning of time.

Each family has a different story, or different variations of the same one. Language, culture, and traditions all seem to make one family experience different from the next, but they are all variations on the same story.

We can look to the stories of the past to bring clarity and a sense of awareness around who we are and how we came to live on the Land we are currently on.

One of the stories that has remained alive in my family is of my Great-Great-Grandmother, who boarded a ship from Ireland with her husband and six sons, suffered an arduous journey, and arrived in what is now referred to as "Canada" as both a grieving widow and mother of three lost sons. Half of her children had died, and she was left without means of support for herself and her three remaining sons, all living in a strange land, and one that was not welcoming to the Irish.

Why did she and her family leave? What were they leaving behind when they came here? I could feel the immensity of that decision and its accompanying journey only to a small *degree when I was living for two years in a trailer far from many of my family members and friends, traveling to places that I had never been. I thought daily about their journey, and what they must have endured.*

My ancient ancestors of hundreds and thousands of years ago lived in harmony with the Earth and other beings. There was an honour and integrity among the Men, and a reverence for the Oracle held in the wombs of the Women.

I learned how to reconnect with my Ancestors and their wisdom through my deep connection to the Moon, her Wisdom, and the Cyclical Living approach that I share about in this book, as well as through courageously facing the shadows that I had hidden away inside, out of fear and shame. Our Ancestors are waiting for us to connect and remember them, keeping their stories and Spirits with us as we move through life and passing them on to future generations. When I first had the intention of re-establishing a connection with my Ancestors, and listening to their guidance, I found some clues to my family's past that brought me a sense of Wholeness- my mother's line is woven with Dark Feminine Medicine and my father's line carries the Wisdom and knowledge of fine craftsmen. Much of this has been forgotten, but it need not be lost.

We can weave a new story from the remnants of cloth that have been left behind, unearthing the statues and stories of the past, and placing them back on the Altar of our collective hearts.

We can pay close attention to our hands, and to the things we make with them, to how we weave our own story, and with whom we weave it.

We can bake the bread and turn the spindles.
We can build houses and grow our own food.

We can take off the masks that we have been wearing out of fear of being truly seen, and we can use our voices, singing the songs of the ones who walked barefoot through the woods, and swam naked in the riverbeds, long before our names were spoken into existence.

We can lift the veil between ourselves and our ancestors, and find peace in remembrance, feeling their wisdom and Love in all that we do, guiding us forward, encouraging each step.

We can wake up to oppressive systems, let go of what does not serve, and rebuild what is good.

Reflections

- What are the gifts that your ancestors (known or unknown) have given to you that you carry in you today?

- What is it that you would like to thank your ancestors for?

- What challenges from your ancestors are you carrying?

- What would you like to have more of in your life that your ancestors enjoyed, and where do you feel there is a piece that's missing?

- What would you like to release that your ancestors either gave to you, or that they didn't pass on to you?

" *This is our meditation practice as women, calling back the dead and dismembered aspects of ourselves, calling back the dead and dismembered aspects of life itself. The one who re-creates from that which has died is always a double-sided archetype. The creation Mother is always also the Death Mother and vice versa. Because of this dual nature, or double tasking, the great work before us is to learn to understand what around and about us and what within us must live, and what must die. Our work is to apprehend the timing of both; to allow what must die to die, and what must to live.* " ~ *Clarissa Pinkoles Estés*

Retained Wisdom
Finding A New Rhythm After Moon-pause

As the Crone or Wise Woman feeds the roots of Rebirth, she is a force for new life, new energy, and closely related to the Maiden. She embodies the previous seasons that come before winter, and this gives her a unique perspective in guiding us when we feel lost or uncertain of the path forward. When death has visited us in any form, and we have gone through the grieving and rest that is necessary for our spiritual change and transformation to occur, like the butterfly still in the chrysalis, we will eventually outgrow the cocoon and be ready to re-enter the world anew. The Wise Woman shows us the way to traverse astral planes of transformation with reverence and a sense of awe for the mystery of life. Reflecting on those things that brought us so much joy as young children and Maidens before we entered our Mother phase can deliver insight to what may spark our interest now.

Demetra George writes in _Mysteries of the Dark Moon_:

"It is a time when a woman, free from the responsibility of raising her family, can enjoy greater freedom, independence, and control of her life. The initiation of widowhood carries the promise of once again having one's life to oneself after passing through the grief of mourning. Travel, continuing education, community service, creative self-expression, occupation change, and spiritual development are some of the avenues that can open unencumbered to The Crone. All *the woman's vital force can now be channeled into giving life and form to her mental and spiritual children. As The Crone confronts the changes in her body and transformations in her lifestyle, she realizes that her old identity is indeed dying. She may be at loss of what to do next and how to go about doing it. It may have been so long since she focused on her own needs and desires that she may have forgotten how to do so. Thus, she may feel ill equipped to face the challenges of this next phase of her life. In order for our Crones to fully actualize the potentials available, we all must confront and dissolve the huge barriers that the patriarchy has con-structed to keep older Women poor, powerless, lonely, un-employable, unconfident, helpless, and ill."*

When any phase ends in our life, it is The Crone who ushers us into the underground caverns of letting go, into the dark spaces where things go to die, to become compost, and to be reborn anew when the timing is right. She is an impenetrable force, as she represents both Death and the soil of Rebirth in the cycle of all life. Whether we try to avoid meeting her and resist the changes that she represents, or whether we fully and openly embrace her in her Wisdom, we can trust that she will beckon to us at some point, when transformation is most needed, and perhaps cannot be avoided.

For those Women who are beyond bleeding, who have passed through this important initiatory phase of the macro cycle of life, this can be celebrated and seen as the beginning of a new way of being in the body; a skin has been shed and a new life can begin. Welcoming new projects that feel exciting and joyful, learning a new craft or skill, being part of and creating spaces that keep sacred practices and ceremony alive – these are all ways to channel life force energy that is still retained in the body, waiting to be used.

What if the answer to greater vitality and wellness for Women as we age is to never stop using that creative life force?

What if dis-ease and end-of-life health issues could all be traced back to a Woman not fully using (or not being allowed to use) her life force energy, for herself in her becoming, and on a larger scale for the greater good of our planet?

Reflections

- What are some beliefs and attitudes that you have about your body / Women's bodies? What are some beliefs about what your body / a Woman's body actually *is*, vs. what it is *not*? What do you believe that your body/ a Woman's body *is* intended for, and what is it *not* meant for? Where do you think that the above beliefs and attitudes about your body / Women's bodies stem from?

- If some kinds of Women's bodies are viewed as being "worth" more, more worthy, or desirable than others' Women's bodies, what does that say about the values held? And what does it say about our place in the world?

- How can you help support Women in general, or a specific Woman in particular, so that the legacy of Wisdom can be left that will enrich the societal soil, and benefit the future? What are some ways that you think that you might leave your own legacy?

Crone Medicine for Those Who Bleed

As we looked at earlier, in both the Maiden / Inner Spring phase, and the Mother / Inner Summer phase, there is upward-moving energy, and estrogen and testosterone are increasing, bringing with them a feeling of more energy to focus on external needs like family, sex with partners, livelihood, caring for others, and being social.

In the second half of the cycle, in both the Wild Woman / Inner Autumn phase, and the Wise Woman / Winter phase, there is a shift to downward-moving energy toward the Earth. Our lower energy centers, where large amounts of life force energy are stored in the womb and pussy, become more active and alive, creating an energy vortex of primal pleasure and raw expression. Sex is focused more on self than with partners, except for unions where lovers are deeply intuitive and giving. This focuses energy inward and down, creating an opportunity to clear stagnant energy, in the womb and in the sacred passageway of the yoni, through the purifying passage of the Wild Woman, and finally the deep, deep Wisdom of the Crone. Here, in this liminal space between what was and what is to be, is the pure potential to create the life we desire.

For those still in their bleeding years, the Crone can offer so much insight during bleeding time, helping us to see clearly the path forward, what is aligned and misaligned, what needs to die, and what needs our attention to grow to fullness.

How can Women who are in the bleeding phases of life learn from the Crone and anchor into her Wisdom, especially if there are few elders (or even none) around to offer guidance and support?

As we approach the end of our bleeding years, we can reflect on two earlier phases of our life - when we were in our early childhood and adolescence (pre-bleeding) years, as well as when we were pregnant and/or nursing - to reveal the knowledge and meaning of those phases, and to draw up the inner supports that we need to make the transition to our beyond-bleeding years, offering us a different way of being in the new phase.

We can remember that our blood holds the remembrance of ancient Feminine Wisdom practices to help us create the new way forward.

We can reach out to other Women for support, especially those who have walked this path ahead of us, gather in Circle and share our stories.

And we can listen to our bodies deeply during bleeding time to truly know the gifts that are waiting there for us to uncover.

Reflections

- What fears arise when you think about your beyond-bleeding/Crone/Wise Woman years?

- What beliefs do you hold about Women as we age, and the aging process in general, that are not serving you?

- What are the common beliefs or opinions about Women and aging in your family?

- What are your current beliefs about aging and sex? Do you believe that sex can be even more Pleasure filled as Women age?

- Are there ways that you can rest and receive more in your life, especially during bleeding time, that will give you a greater sense of Wholeness?

- When have you felt the Crone energy of death and endings most present in your life and what medicine did she offer as you journeyed back into the rebirth phase?

Sweet Rest ~ A Visit from My Ancestors

Will you rest when there's no more to do?
That simply can't be
There's always an excuse
In that way of thinking

Will you rest when your bones are so weary from carrying
you around?
When your feet can no longer move
When your body hits the ground
Too tired to even make a sound?

Will you rest when winter comes?
Beckoning at your door
Snowy drifts, windy shifts
When the leaves have disappeared
Decaying on the forest floor

Under the snow
a blanket of peace
Whispers of quiet times
Letting go of brighter times?

If this isn't a sign for us -
What is?

There'll always be a summer after this
I promise

But now.

Akaiy'ha

Rest and come down to your roots
It's heavy and earthy down here
And we miss you

Ancestors calling your name
Veils thinning out
Come back down
We need you here in the dark
hollows of the ground

Spring will come and call our names back out
There'll be plenty of space for doing

Rest now sweet soul
Be still and surrender to the death of it all
For without death
Life cannot be

Free Bleeding

There is no shame is letting
the rivers of your blood flow, Sister
Make it ceremony
Free bleed on the Altar of animal skin
Soak your clothes in the sink
and let the water run Red
Get into the tub with your yoni dripping Earth Nectar
and bathe in your beauty
Adorn your face
Paint a pussy picture with your blood
Let your lover lick you clean

Womb Lodge

As Women in tribal cultures, we would regularly step outside of the general community of our tribe, and gather together with the rest of the Women, to create beautiful things, to sing, dance, nourish our bodies, share stories, and listen to each other's wisdom.

Being raised under the pervasive influence of patriarchal, hierarchical, colonial systems can make gathering with other Women in this intimate way feel intimidating and overwhelming. The womb (along with the heart) holds the keys to healing the wounds that have separated Women from the Feminine.

Our womb spaces are like large bowls, intended for carrying and holding babies, holding the water of life, much like the baskets we carried in ancient times to gather water or medicine. We are not made to withstand isolation for long periods of time, and the circular rhythm of life reminds us of this. Like a basket shows us, we are strongest when our individual lives are woven together; our hearts and spirits grounded in our medicine and truth.

A womb lodge is where healing can happen for Women. In the past, and still to this day, it has been called the "Red Tent" and "Bleeding Lodge" or "Moon Lodge"; I prefer to call it a *Womb Lodge*.

The womb lodge is a place for Women to gather to mark the time of Menarche and other sacred passageways, for ritual, ceremony, and celebration – a space where life is witnessed through the body, the seasons are celebrated in their ever-changing wholeness, and we are witnessed in our full spectrum of living; all are welcome as a blessing to the whole. It is a place for Women to let things go, to detach from energies that are feeling heavy and burdensome, and to allow our blood to cleanse us of what is no longer needed for the journey ahead. It provides a container for us to gather, share, and hold each other through life seasons, or anytime that we feel called to listen to other Women with greater intent, and to hear the Wisdom held within our vessel.

There is a pulse in Mother Earth and a pulse that lives in our Womb Space. It is akin to a heartbeat or a drumbeat. As we come into spaces that are shared with other Women, the beating grows louder and stronger - the collective echo of the connected beating of the Earth and the heart-womb that lives in each Woman. Below you will find guidance for creating your own Womb Lodge at home or in a space with other Women.

Creating a Womb Lodge

We can create a womb lodge space that is meant just for ourselves, or we can create one that is intended to be shared in gatherings with our Sisters.

Whether we still bleed, or whether we are beyond-bleeding in our life cycle, we may wish to create a personal womb lodge for ourselves in our home, where we can take a sacred pause for a day, several days, or even a week each month, go inward, and pay attention to our deepest needs for letting go, rest, and rejuvenation. This can be a personal space where any Woman can simply BE, reflect on what has been, gather Wisdom, and release what is no longer needed.

The intention matters when creating a womb lodge that will be either just for yourself, or for gatherings of Women.

Whether for personal or Circle use, you can reflect on the questions below. If you are co-creating a womb lodge, gather with your Sisters to do the exercise as a group, recording every piece of the puzzle, until it becomes clear what you intend to create together.

Individually and/or as a group, make a list of the ideas, words, and visions that come to mind when you feel into what you want to birth or create within this space. Be as detailed as you like.

Some questions you may wish to consider, if appropriate for

the situation, are:

- What is the purpose of this space?
- How do I/ we want the space to feel?
- How do I / we want others to feel in this space?
- What kind of healing practices will be offered or shared here?
- Will there be regular gatherings?
- Will they be in sync with The Moon's cycles, and in what way?

If you have decided to create your own womb lodge, start by finding a space in your home or outdoors that feels supportive and nurturing, where you can lie down comfortably. This could be somewhere that is darker, to support the energies of death, rest, and rejuvenation.

Maybe you already have an Altar space where you can come to for this practice, but, if not, decide where one could be. Place an altar cloth, candles, crystals, bones, dried flowers or herbs, your menstrual blood, items that represent Winter or Crone/ Wise Woman energy for you, oils that you may use throughout your practice (or ones that are specifically for the cycle you are in), arranging them based on your intuition.

You may wish to incorporate the four elements, directions, or seasons as you feel called. For example, you may wish to incorporate the element of water by taking a bath or shower (warm is best as it balances cooling Crone energy) or by having a bowl of water on the Altar. Another example might be including the element of fire, the flame of a candle, to honour the passing of the torch from Wild Woman to Crone as bleeding time begins, or from Crone to Maiden as the bleeding ends.

For more tips on Altar Creation, see the section on page 232.

Gather whatever you may need to make this time feel supportive. This could be making yourself a cup of tea, having your favourite book nearby, playing gentle music - everything to experience deep self-nurturing.

What you eat is an important part of caring for your womb and the rest of your body during this time, as well as during all parts of your cycle. Eating foods that are rich in iron and other blood-fortifying nutrients will help your body through this time, and ensure you have energy for the cycle ahead. There is nowhere else that you need to go, and nothing else you need to do; you are here as a witness to honour this liminal space between death and rebirth.

How to Sit in Circle at a Sisters' Womb Lodge

You and your Sisters can create a womb lodge together that feels supportive and safe. Remember that there is no "right" or "wrong" way to sit in Circle as Women, but there are some ways that can feel more supportive than others, especially as we are in a time of undoing harmful patriarchal, colonial systems.

Here are a few ways we can be deeply present with each other in Circle, ways that will continue to draw us back together, over and over again:

1. Place objects on the Altar that evoke the Goddess, and invite your Sisters to bring items for the altar, as well;
2. State expectations around confidentiality, listening deeply with compassion, speaking in turn
3. Suggest that any judgment that comes up be something that is used to reflect on oneself
4. Point out that the Circle has no apex, no beginning nor end, so no one is at the head of it, and every Woman is as valuable as any other
5. Listen for the sake of listening - not to give advice, just to be present, and allow each of your Sisters to be heard
6. Speak your Truth, allowing yourself to be vulnerable and authentic
7. Ask for what you need in terms of support and be open to receiving
8. Talk about the seasons of a Woman's life and share your insights with each other
9. Talk about your monthly cycles

10. Spend some time in silence and breathing together
11. Sing Medicine Songs/ Ancestral Songs that ignite and honour Goddess energy, breathing back air into her lungs
12. Dance and move your bodies, letting it flow intuitively, without needing to follow steps
13. Get Naked and shake your bodies to some deep beats
14. Steam your wombs and pussies, tending to your sacred gardens
15. Read stories or poetry, or make art
16. Hold a *Fire Release Ceremony* (outlined on page 190 of this book)
17. Share food through potluck contributions
18. Explore the endless possibilities to let connection, Joy and Pleasure in!

Altar Creation

An Altar is a tangible and visual representation of the combination of our inner world, the spirit world, and the outer world. It brings together what matters most to us, what is most sacred, with our desires and visions for what we wish to create and call in. It can be created at any point in our cycle and/or The Moon's cycle, and it can be changed at any point - when we feel called to shift the energy of a particular area of our life, or when we want a space to honour any part of the birth-death-rebirth cycle. There is no right or wrong way to do this. Allow your intuition to guide you and get creative with it!

- Find a space in your home or outdoors where you wish to place an Altar for Ritual or Ceremony, preferably a space that will not be disrupted.

- You may wish to explore the various shapes of Altars as well. Will your Altar be circular, triangular, square, at the front of an area or back, surrounding a tree or sacred spot in nature? The shape that feels the best for you is the right one, and may also be a combination of a few various shapes, or a sacred geometric pattern.

- You may wish to call in your Ancestors by saying a prayer or meditation to bless the space such as: "I call in my Ancestors and their wisdom to guide me in this Altar setting, to bless this space with their Love and remembrance. May this be a space of devotion and Love toward all beings and for the Earth. And so it is." You may also wish to use the Ancestral Healing Prayer as part of your Altar Creation Ceremony, which can be found on page 235.

- Select objects that have special significance to you. These could be candles, crystals, flowers, Goddess statues and images representing the Sacred Feminine, herbs or wands for smoke cleansing, bones, tarot or oracle cards, and any items representing what you are desiring to call in, in this phase. Bringing in the energy of the elements of Air, Water, Earth, and Fire can also support this process. Take a moment with each object to feel into the energy it holds, using your intuition to guide you as to where it should be placed on the Altar.

- Select items that represent the season or the archetype you wish to work with, or the energy you wish to call in to help with release and healing. For instance, in the Maiden phase, you may wish to bring in items that represent a sense of youth and newness, like seeds or sprouts; for the Mother, you could choose items that imbue your space with fullness and growth like fresh flowers or herbs; for the Wild Woman, feature dried flowers or items representing decay and letting go, and; for the Crone/ Wise Woman, offer bones or fossils. These are some examples, but use your intuition to guide you.

- Bring any Medicines that you are currently working with and learning from into the Altar space, as it shows reverence and respect for their teachings, recognizes their gifts, and honours them as teachers and allies. In some lineages, it is not recommended to place Medicine on the ground. It is wise to ask around in your community and do some research beforehand, so you know best practices. If you are without this guidance (as many are), ask for guidance from the Medicine itself, tuning into the energy of the plants and flowers, and listen to the answer before moving forward. Trust that what comes through is perfect and right for you at this time.

- Lighting a candle on the Altar invites in the energy of transformation and light. This can be a powerful focal point for the Altar space, and a place where you can sit and meditate or pray when you feel called.

Akaiy'ha

Ancestral Healing Prayer

I call upon my sacred ancestors to guide, direct, and sur-round me in loving protection.

I ask for your guidance and support,
To help me see clearly what I cannot see,
To help me find the way forward where I feel lost,
To remind me how sacred and perfect all of life is,
To hold me through grief and loss of the old,
To help me soften into new ways and welcome the new,
To give me courage and strength to pursue my dreams that sometimes seem too much for my logical mind to grasp,
To show me the way of ease and beauty that is always there.

I ask that you guide me into spaces where my spirit will fly freely, and without shame or judgment, from myself or others.

I ask for protection from energies that would wish me harm.

I ask for protection from energies that are not aligned with my truest purpose in this lifetime.
I ask for protection from energies that put greed above peace, and war above Love.

I ask for support and strength to carry the wishes and dreams of my ancestors forward, to build what has been dreamt of in my lineage and spoken about for thousands of years into existence.

I offer this prayer of gratitude to all my ancestors for their lives lived.
I offer this prayer of gratitude for the lessons I have learned, and the wisdom I have uncovered through these lessons.
I offer prayers of Love and devotion to my ancestral lines for reconciling and repairing what has been broken.
I offer prayers of devotion to the path of Love and remembrance of the old ways and new ways in sacred union.

I open myself to receiving all of the Love from my ancestors into my womb space, into my being, into the Oneness of creation.

I open my heart to allowing grief, heartaches, loss, loneliness, and despair to flow through me, and to inviting warmth, tenderness, Gratitude, and Joy to reside more fully within me.

The rivers of change are within me, and I allow them to flow freely, without control, without building a dam to keep anything in, without holding back any of who I am.

I allow
I allow
I allow

I receive
I receive

I receive

And so it is.

With great gratitude for my ancestors and their teachings, I remain open to receiving their wisdom and guidance now.

I am open to receive your Love and guidance
I am open to receive your Love and guidance
I am open to receive your Love and guidance

And so it is.

Moon Blood Ceremony

A Moon Blood Ceremony is a practice of reverence for the birth-death-rebirth cycle. It is an honouring of the sacred blood that flows through us and out of us, back to the Great Mother Earth.

In our modern over-culture, we have become accustomed to flushing our blood down the toilet or throwing it into the trash on a blood soaked tampon or a disposable pad. Not only does this create unnecessary garbage and toxic waste for our beloved Earth home, but it also speaks to the disregard that we have for our menstrual blood and its healing properties.

Instead, Women can offer up a Moon Blood Offering Prayer (see below), along with gratitude to the Earth, and then present our blood as a gift to the Earth, either by pouring it from a container where it was collected earlier, or by squatting to bleed onto the Earth. This doesn't mean that every time we need to release or go to the toilet, that instead, we need to go outside, as this may not be realistic for our modern lifestyles. But, it is an invitation to consider something that maybe we haven't previously, to consider that our blood comes from Mother Earth, and that it is our way of re-establishing a loving connection with her and our bodies as a practice, when we feel called, or when it is available to us. Even offering our blood once per cycle is a powerful way to say Thank You and honour this connection.

Perhaps a tree is calling you to it, or you are drawn to a mossy patch in the forest. Maybe you feel a deep connection to a body of water, like the ocean or a lake, and you would like to release your blood there, with prayers and offerings.

Follow your intuition, allowing your creative juices to flow as to how you offer and honour your menstrual blood. When it comes with an intention from the heart, there are no right or wrong ways to do this, remembering that the heart and womb are so deeply connected and support each other in a never- ending loop within the vessels of our being.

Akaiy'ha

Moon Blood Offering Prayer

Sacred Earth
beneath my feet
I offer my blood back to you

Wild Earth
where all roots meet
The death of the old
gives birth to the new

Prayer to the Great Mother

I speak this prayer into existence for the Great Mother. May these words be seeds in her womb, creating a ripple-effect out into the world.

I am a vessel of unconditional Love and support for the Earth, for the Great Mother, for her children - plant, animal, sea creature, insect, bird, human kin - all who have been born from her womb.
I offer my Love in service, to protect and uphold peace and sovereignty on this earthly plane, and for all who inhabit here.

I am a force of Nature, created by the Great Mother, born from her wind which fills my lungs and shapes my songs, her fire which fuels my will to live and beats my heart, her water which feeds my body Earth vessel and aligns me to the seasons, and her soil which grounds me in the presence of her unconditional Love.

My body is my home while here, the space of sacred ritual and remembrance.

I pray to the Great Mother that I devote my words, actions, and thoughts to being in loving union with my body.

I pray to the Great Mother that I be a vessel of unconditional Love and support for the healing and growth of the planet Earth and her inhabitants.

I pray to the Great Mother that I be of clear mind, receptive body, and loving heart, and that I may serve from this awareness.

I pray to the Great Mother that I have the courage and strength to know when to let go of harmful habits that keep me hidden or small, out of fear.

I release myself from any hold that harmful habits have had on me, reclaiming my full sovereignty, of mind, body, and spirit.

The Great Mother knows and recognizes me as a sovereign being, and I see myself as she sees me.

I see myself as she sees me.
I see myself as she sees me.
I see myself as she sees me.
And so it is.

Wild Joy

What is the true gift of the Wild Woman, of calling back all lost and forgotten parts of ourselves, and restoring them to wholeness?

Joy.
Unbound
Untethered
Unleashed
Pure Ecstatic Joy.

It took me a while to make the link between my untamed Wild expression and Joy. I had to go through the layers, like peeling back layers of an onion, and let the natural flow take its course, through feeling it all the way back to the beginning.

I discovered a place inside of myself that existed beyond all of these pathways and feelings, a place so pure and innocent it brought me to my knees, humbled me to my core. It was a place of pure void and potentiality, the place I was created from.

What arose from this was a remembrance that I had, indeed, experienced this before, through a memory that resurfaced during my Wild Woman Reclamation- on the day of my birth, on the day my parents first held me, and looked at my face, and I at theirs, a day that showed me that I was Love embodied.

I had that same feeling of Wild Joy, all the way back to the moment I was born.

The beginning of a cycle comes after the ending of a previous one. And there is space, in the "between", for us to collect ourselves fully before moving on, to honour what was, before starting the next thing, to pay attention to the ongoing cycle that all of life on Earth moves through day to day, moon to moon, year to year, a cycle without end.

The Wild Woman shows us what it is to let go of habitual patterns that are keeping us stuck on a wheel that feels like it is out of alignment. It is like driving a car with one wheel that is not quite right; the car is getting pulled to one side, even right off of the road for a reason. *It's up to us to stop and pay attention.*

Wild Woman is here to remind us that we always have choice, that we are not victims of our reality; our souls came here to play, to create, and to experience deep, profound amounts of Joy and Pleasure. The Wild Woman's howl is one of calling back those parts of ourselves we need to make life's whole mystical, magickal ride worthwhile, to live the full spectrum of our being, and to dance with wild abandon, without a thought about who is watching - and especially when they might be!

She implores us to stop listening to voices that are not our own, to pay attention to the world around us and within us, and to be a force of Love on the planet through the Dark Feminine energy that is so needed in the collective right now.

The Wild Woman is an activist for Joy, in the greatest sense. Joy is the reason for her actions, as she knows the way to our hearts, wombs, and pussies, and how to awaken and invigorate us with renewed vitality and purpose.

The Wild Woman is the key that so many of us Women have been searching for, to unlock those parts of ourselves and let them all come out to play - unashamedly, in the open. She is the bridge between upper and lower, left and right, outside and inside, and she resides in the collective heart-womb of our being.

Joy is the result of living without resistance to the natural flow of life, to our natural rhythms and cycles. The natural world is Joy, the heart of life in movement.

We get stuck in thinking that we need to hide something as natural and as beautiful as aging, that we need to alter our appearance to suit an over-culture's values and desires. We may feel that we are expected to do all we can to stand out and fit in - primp and prime, fluff and fill - a never-ending to-do and to-buy list of things to alter ourselves, deny who we are, fill the void inside of us, and create yet a larger barrier between ourselves and nature.

When will we stop and pay attention?

When nature is out of balance, it seeks to bring itself back into balance. The more out of balance, the longer the distance needing to be traveled to get back to harmony.

When I close my eyes and try to imagine what the world would be like if the Wild Woman didn't exist, I see a vast landscape of nothingness, a barren ground, war torn, gray and lifeless. I see no signs of life, no colour, no movement. I see nothing that is worth living for.

To remove "Wild" from Woman is like removing wings from a butterfly; it might resemble a caterpillar, but not one unfolded into the fullness of its being.

And when we learn to dance with Wild Woman, and let her take the lead, guiding us toward deeper Pleasure and Wild Joy, she teaches us HOW.

We can attune ourselves to the cycle of The Moon, and let her be our guide, regardless of where we are at in our life cycle - at any age, any time. When tuned in, we naturally know and feel when it is time to plant seeds, grow, birth, and harvest, and when to turn inwards for reflection and rest. We can live the cycle fully and wholly, giving ourselves over to it, trusting in the perfection of the life matrix that created every being and process on Earth. We can trust that life is so fucking juicy, warm, and soft, and sweet beyond our wildest dreams, when we do all of the things that elicit a FULL BODY "YES!"

Final Word

Dear Sister,

It is inevitable that, if you've come this far, resting now at the end of this journey and the beginning of your next, you have come to know the Wild Woman who lives in you more deeply. You have come to listen to her, and perhaps to hear her, as she howls and cries for your attention, and also to appreciate her for her profound and truly raw and unique expression. And by "her", I actually mean YOU, dear Sister.

If this book and our journey together is to bear fruit, let it be this.....

Let it be a *waking up* of any dormant, sleeping parts of your existence, and a calling to reintegrate them into your Sacred, Wild Being.

Let it be a *remembering* of who you truly are, and a promise that you will always make space for all that you are, and all you will continue to be.

Let it be a *Wild and Blissful* passageway to your Wisdom and Sacred Medicine.

Let it be a *Call to Action* to live in the most free and authentic way you can, without delay or hindrance and to serve from this place in whatever you do.

Let it be a *Joyous Bellowing* out to your Sisters, near and far, to come and have Tea at your place, and share stories in Circle.

Let it be a *Journey* free of shame, guilt, and blame, where you can spread your wings and fly anywhere your heart desires, with anyone you choose.

Let it be a *Sacred Homecoming* back to Ancestral Wisdom and Sisterhood.

Let it be a *Rooting Back into the Womb* of the Great Mother Earth, and a blossoming of your greatest potential and gifts.

It is true that there was a time when the Dark Goddess and her Wild Women Sisters were banished and exiled, hidden away and buried. And there was a time when we, too, had to learn to conceal those parts of ourselves, out of fear and self-protection.

But NOW is not that time.

NOW is the time of *Wild Reclamation* that is *within* each of us, and that is *for all of us*.

All stars and planets point to this truth. I know you feel it. Why?

Because YOU ARE IT.
You carry the Sacred Medicine of Remembrance in your Womb.

Sister, I ask you...

If not NOW, then WHEN?

If not YOU, then WHO?
WE need your Medicine.

WE need YOU.

LET US SEE YOU, HEAR YOU, AND BE THERE FOR YOU –
WITH YOU!

Give yourself permission to DANCE NAKED in WILD
,UNTAMED ABANDON and let yourself know endless and
profound PLEASURE.

HEART HUMMING
WOMB PULSING
PUSSY DRIPPING
TOE CURLING
P L E A S U R E
...
SISTER, IT IS CLEAR.

There is no better time than NOW

to UNLEASH YOUR WILD.

Acknowledgements

Most babies – whether little humans, or creative projects made by humans – are fortunate to have compassionate, nurturing, loving care during their births. This "baby" – this book – was no exception, and it could not, and would not, have been brought so beautifully to life, as it is now, if not for the many kind souls who made its birth possible.

It is with immense Joy and Honour that I offer deep, heartfelt Thanks and Gratitude to some very important Women who helped this baby come to life in the world – Women who felt into my vision, wove their own magick through, and created a shared fabric and network of Sacred expression that exists between these two covers.

Firstly, to my dear Sister and a brilliant mind, Wen Fiadh Cerys: You gave so generously of your time and energy by conducting research, providing all levels of editing, and magickly massaging the manuscript, as well as by offering an abundance of Sisterly Love, Crone Wisdom, and listening. If this book is a baby, and I am her Mother, then you, Wen, are the GrandMother. Your courage to listen, share, and open me up to expressing things that were difficult to talk and write about, was an immense gift that I will cherish for a lifetime. Thank You, Wen.

Next, there are two Women whose artistic expressions grace the pages and cover of this book.

To Treese Moore: You are a brilliant graphic artist, drawing and hand-painting the many Wheels needed to support content in this book. Your use of details and fun graphics imbued the words and teachings with so much vibrancy and depth, beyond what words could do alone. Thank You, Treese. (You can find her holding Kasba Women's Circles on Vancouver Island with her daughter. She can be reached at beeskneesbnb@gmail.com or on IG @funwithtreese)

To Jeanne Beaudry: I fell in love with your work the moment I saw it, and I couldn't help but feel the same way about you the moment that we connected about working together on this creation. Through your intuition and talented hands, your stunning illustrations now punctuate this book - the Wolf Woman, Wolves Dancing, Sacred Union, Self-Pleasure Goddess, and the animals and waves seen throughout, as well as the front cover illustration of Earth Priestess. Each drawing that came through was even more gorgeous than the one before it, capturing the essence of the words so beautifully. Thank You, Jeanne. (You can find out more about Jeanne's offerings and work on her website: http://www.jeannebeaudryartetyoga.com)

To my amazing team of publishers, the Women-led team of Samantha Moonsammy and Simar Nounou at Lucky Book Publishing: You were instrumental in helping this baby make her debut in the world. Your savvy skills and knowledge of the publishing world made the process easy and fluid, and the Author's Community you have brilliantly created provided me, and others like me, with the stamina needed for that one final push. Thank You, Samantha and Simar.

To C. Ketani Plewes: You cheered me on as I addressed some difficult issues in this book, and you inspired me with your work in sharing Indigenous Culture and Tradition. I am deeply grateful for your kindness and Love, Ketani.

This book contains not just my own story, but the story of many Women who share similar, resonating experiences and views on life. To the hundreds of Women who have sat with me over the years, you have shared your stories and opened your hearts to me and to the other Women, both in Circle and in Private Sessions. Your stories have left an imprint on my Heart, Womb, and Spirit. I am grateful to you for listening to my shares, for holding space for me, for witnessing my grand unfolding into my Wild Sacred Self. Your Wisdom, Courage, Softness, and Strength have shown me a new way forward; healing and Wholeness are, indeed, possible, not just for me, but for all of us Women who wish to claim it. THANK YOU, SISTERS.

To my beautiful Children: I cannot imagine that this life would be nearly as magickal without you, or that my purpose would be as fueled by passion and purpose if you had not chosen me to be your Mother in this lifetime. Your births and your beings have opened me up to new ways of experiencing my body, and you shone a light on those parts of myself that I had been hiding, guiding me back home. Thank You, my Loves.

What baby can be born without the Sacred Seed of the Divine Masculine? To my Wild Man, Luke: My life made a pivotal turn on that fateful night when our souls danced together in the ethers and our bodies became Lovers in Sacred Union. I had no idea what the future had in store, nor that I would eventually be writing about that night, and our other Wild adventures together. To use your words, "You have shown me a deeper love than I have ever known" - or even that I thought was possible. You, my Love, have shown me that Sacred Union is not only possible, but necessary for living a life where we wake up electrified to live fully each day. Your Love and unwavering devotion have shown me a new way of seeing the Masculine; it has provided a salve to the wounds that were present when we met. You have never once made me feel like my Wild couldn't exist in your realm. You have been unconditional in your acceptance and Love of all that I am and all that I bring to the world. You have witnessed me in my "deepest sorrow and most ravenous rage", never flinching once. My love for you is deep as the Ocean and as vast as the Cosmos. For being the most incredible provider and support system that I have ever known - Thank You, Luke.

One last note, this to my Ancestors: You traversed the astral planes and moved through the roots of the trees to find me walking alone in desolate places; when I felt nobody cared, you were there with me. I recognize now that it was you all along, all of you, who wrote so much of this book through me and beside me, guiding me back home to the Old Ways - for Healing, for Love, and for Wholeness. Thank You, Ancient Ones.

About the Author

Akaiy'ha is a Sacred Feminine Embodiment Guide, Wisdom Holder of the Old Ways, and Birther of New Ways. Her offerings are a bridge for others, guiding them back Home to their Wild Ancestral Hearts. Her Ceremonial approach in her offerings combine teachings brought forward through her Ancestral and Celtic Heritage, as well as those she has learned and been given through her deep connection to Nature, Mother Earth, and Grandmother Moon. She is Founder of Medicine Women Rising, a Community of Women who also are bridges and leaders in their communities, collectively empowering and uplifting Women Worldwide. She hosts Retreats and Trainings in Womb Wisdom, Ancestral Healing, and Sexual Sovereignty in various parts of the world, gathers Women for The Way of The Wild Women Festival, and is the Mother of Wümlodge - a gathering space for Women to sing, dance, sit in Circle, and rejoice in their Feminine vessels. For more information about offerings, including any current and upcoming events, or to connect with Akaiy'ha, please visit www.medicinewomenrise.com

MY GIFT TO YOU!

I am so glad you're here!

As my Gift to you, get FREE Access to Audio Recordings of several Practices as well as Printable PDFs of the Wheels found throughout the book and other Free Resources by scanning the QR Code below or visiting https://medicinewomenrise.com/free-resources-signup/

---

thank you

THANK YOU FOR READING MY BOOK

I really appreciate all of your feedback and I love hearing what you have to say.

Please leave a helpful review on Amazon letting me know what you thought of the book.

Thanks so much!

Akaiy'ha

www.ingramcontent.com/pod-product-compliance
Lightning Source LLC
Chambersburg PA
CBHW070103030426
42335CB00016B/1988